BREAKING VASES

BREAKING
VASES

Shattering Limitations &
Daring to Thrive:
A Middle Eastern
Woman's Story

Dima Ghawi

Published in the United States of America by Dima Ghawi, LLC
First edition, 2017
Requests for permission to reproduce material from this work should be sent to: info@breakingvases.com

Library of Congress Control Number: 2017959517
ISBN 978-0-9978093-5-0 (print)

Publishing:
Project management by Gretchen Otto, Motto Publishing Services
Writing coaching, developmental editing, and writing assistance by Herpreet Singh
Final revisions by Francesca Crozier-Fitzgerald
Copyediting by Cynthia Lindlof
Proofreading by Monique LeBlanc
Cover design and interior art by Jessica Weimer O'Connor
Interior design by Amber Morena

Discounts for bulk sales are available:
contact info@breakingvases.com

CONTENTS

DEDICATION

"Kiddo, you are doing great." No matter the subject, every time we speak, Uncle Anton says these words to me. Regardless of whether it's related to education, business, or any risk I take, Uncle Anton is the first person I call with good or bad news.

When I was a little girl, he traveled from the United States to our hometown of Amman, Jordan, for visits. When he arrived at our home, he used to stand with his feet grounded, his arms open, and a huge smile between his well-groomed black mustache and beard. The second I saw him, I used to run to him, and he threw his arms around me and held me as he laughed. His hugs were a full embrace, like being wrapped in a comfortable blanket. Even now, as I write these words in my forties, Uncle Anton's hugs make me feel like I am wrapped in love.

At one of the lowest points in my life, a week after I left my husband, I called Uncle Anton. I was twenty-four, heartbroken, and terrified. I cried and cried while he listened on the other end of the line. He did not say a word, but I could feel his strong presence and support; it was exactly what I needed. I cried for an hour while he listened quietly.

When I was finally ready to start a conversation, Uncle Anton said, "Dima, in our family, we were raised into a cycle of abuse that has been passed down from one generation to the next. We were taught to accept that cycle and believe that it is the only option for living, even though it continues to hurt us and strips us of our inner power. Trust me, this cycle is not just suppressing the women but the men as well."

"By rejecting a miserable life," he continued, "you are breaking that cycle of abuse for yourself and also stopping it from moving forward to the next generation. Don't look back. Things will eventually work out JUST FINE. Believe in yourself, and you'll be okay. Always know that I will support you."

Three years later, when I completed my MBA, Uncle Anton sent a card with a little something extra and a message: "I am enclosing a blast from the past, hope you like it," he wrote. Inside, I found this letter.

January 24, 1983

Dear Uncle Anton,

How are you and how is Auntie Annette? I hope you are doing well. How is your work? I finished my final exams and I feel happy. Tata, Grandpa, Mama, Baba, Uncle Qader, Waseem, and Auntie Nadia, and Uncle Zaid, and me are very very happy. Waseem is now in Kindergarten and I am in elementary school. Uncle, save this letter for me when I grow up.

Kisses to you and Auntie Annette,
Dima

Over the years, Uncle Anton has sent many of these letters. Opening them feels like opening an old box from childhood and finding a favorite worn-out, stuffed bear. I can see my Arabic handwriting develop over the years, but the messages are similar, reflecting my sheltered life. The letters, like Uncle Anton, remind me of where I came from and also where I am now—living in a world of limitless opportunities.

This book is dedicated to Uncle Anton, who transformed in my life from an uncle to a father figure to a spiritual teacher. He is the hope I carry for the men in our family to continue breaking this cycle.

PROLOGUE
2017

A'ilmu noor wal-jahl thalam is an Arabic saying that means, simply, "Knowledge is light, and ignorance is darkness." When I was a child, an adolescent, and even a young woman, the knowledge I needed to form my identity and a healthy sense of self-worth was presented to me in a mixture with inaccuracies, superstitions, and threats. As a result, I spent much of my youth in the dark.

My father, a respected doctor and the head of a government hospital in Amman, Jordan, was six feet tall, but he seemed even taller to me. When I was growing up, he used to tell me a story. It's one I heard many times.

Baba used to begin, "A ten-year-old Jordanian girl immigrated with her parents to the United States. Shortly after their move, every time her father attempted to discipline his daughter by beating her, the girl would say, 'I am going to call the police if you hit me again.' Her father was patient with her threat."

I hung on his every word, transfixed on his serious green eyes and the way his trim mustache moved above his lips as he spoke.

"The next summer," Baba continued, "her father made plans for the family to visit Jordan. His daughter was excited to see her cousins and friends. So, the man got his family on the plane.

Once they landed in the airport in Amman, he took off his belt and started beating his daughter in front of everyone. 'Call the police, if you can, now,' he told her, as he continued beating her. Then, he never allowed her to go back to the States again."

Was this story true or false? I do not know. But I believed my father completely. I could not predict that one day, I would bring so much shame to him that he would threaten my life.

BREAKING VASES

PART ONE

*A Perfect
Glass Vase*

1   *A Perfect Glass Vase*

M y grandmother's well-worn hands cradled a clear, round vase. She asked, "Do you see this pure, perfect glass?" Tata's tone was serious. Her voice was lower than usual, and her delicate grasp emphasized the vulnerable nature of this object's existence.

I strained my eyes to carefully examine the vase in her hands. Unable to see beyond the obvious, I shifted my gaze to Tata's dark brown eyes; their usual warm spark was missing, and I felt alarmed. It was as if a cloud was blocking the sun that normally shone around her. The room was cold, and for the first time, Tata seemed cold.

I was five years old, and in that moment, standing with my two feet firmly on Tata's kitchen floor in Amman, I was certain the world had stopped spinning. My heart raced. Hoping to reignite her missing, familiar warmth, I nodded.

With her eyes fixed on mine, staring hard into my impressionable soul, Tata said, "A girl is just like this clear, glass vase: if the vase gets cracked for any reason, you can never fix it or glue it back. It will always be seen as cracked."

In the culture of my youth, this story and many similar metaphors have been passed down for generations. Some women are

3

told their reputation is like a mirror: if it gets cracked, they'll wake up every morning and see their own reflection as broken, damaged, and imperfect. The glass vase and mirror both represent a Middle Eastern girl's reputation—symbols of its fragility. Any cracks or blemishes—even the smallest cracks—are considered disastrous and irreversible.

Tata's lesson was an early warning that molded my worldview. She wanted me to understand that my actions would be watched and judged. A crack in my vase would also affect my family's reputation and our small Christian community's perception of me forever. In order to fit in and be respected, I needed to maintain a perfect image.

At that age, what was impossible for me to consider was that cracks in my vase could do so much more than affect my family's reputation—my cracks could create a vibration that would shake all of our foundations and, in turn, crack the vases of others whom I love. What was equally impossible for me to consider was that cracks in our vases could result in good.

"And who would want a cracked vase?" Tata asked me on that day, her voice stern and unwavering as she looked into my young, startled eyes. "That is the one we throw in the trash."

2) The Scent of Gossip

For each step Tata takes, I take two. We walk slowly next to each other on the paved sidewalk. She grips my hand and doesn't let it go, except when we arrive at jasmine vines that climb over the white walls that separate the homes from the city street.

Pausing, Tata looks at each vine and comments on the blooms. "Shikilha ma'bbayeh," it looks full, she'll say, or, "Shikilha fadieh," it looks empty. If a vine is abundant with tiny, beautiful flowers, we stop to pick some and place the buds in the white plastic bag Tata is holding. I rub the first few between my palms and then smell the fresh, sweet aroma on my hands. Tata instructs me to pick jasmine with closed buds, because they'll last longer. But I love to pick the ones that have already bloomed, and before I put them in the bag, I admire their tiny petals.

Each time we come to a house with jasmine spilling over its wall, we stop. As we walk, I fill the bag happily, knowing that later, Tata and I will string these tiny, fragrant flowers into necklaces and bracelets with our needles and a thread.

Between stops, we talk about everything. I share all my secrets with Tata. I tell her about the latest toy that my three-year-old brother, Waseem, has broken. I tell her about my friends and teachers in kindergarten. I describe the doll dresses I want her to sew for me. This is our weekly adventure, and it lasts until we arrive at our destination: Em Yousef's house for a coffee visit.

The front gate is made of iron bars. There are two big plants on either side, and hanging down from one of the bars on a strong, thin string is a big round pendant made of colored glass. It looks like a giant, flattened marble, a disc of Mediterranean blue, white, and aqua-blue, with a black dot in the center. Tata says it deflects the Evil Eye, and it's there to watch over the house and protect the family from the negative energy of envy. Though I see it everywhere, I cannot understand why people use it or how it works. I am scared of how that watchful eye stares at me.

We open the gate and walk through the garden toward the main entrance. Tata rings the bell, and, standing side by side, we wait. I hear older women talking and giggling inside. Mira, Em Yousef's daughter, opens the heavy wooden door and greets us with a smile. My mouth is already watering as she leans down to me, because I know what is coming. She opens her fist to give me a caramel chew. Mira is older than I am. She is in high school, but in my eyes, she dresses and talks like a grown-up. I love to have her attention while Tata and her friends talk.

As we walk to the sitting area, I see the faces of five women, all around Tata's age; they are the same faces that gather each week. The women stand and greet us with hugs and kisses on both cheeks. One of them always puts her hand on top of my head as she asks Tata, "How is Rasha doing?" Rasha is my mom. She works as a secretary for a pharmaceutical company while Tata takes care of Waseem and me.

Without a blink, Tata responds, "Rasha is doing great. She is happily married and busy with her family." Tata knows that isn't entirely true, but she also knows that any cracks must stay hidden.

When we all sit down, Mira brings over a brass tray engraved with beautiful Arabic calligraphy. The tray holds six tiny decorated coffee cups and a matching metal pot of hot Turkish coffee. I love the smell of the coffee, but I am not allowed to try it. If I ask, Tata says, "Dima, aib." For shame. It would be shameful for a little girl to have coffee. I am shy, but I observe these women and listen to everything they say. After Mira pours the coffee and serves the little cups, I hear each woman compliment, "Inshallah nefrah feeki." We hope to celebrate seeing you get married soon, they tell her.

Sitting on a fluffy lambskin carpet like a puppy at Tata's feet, I watch Mira blush and smile with satisfaction.

On one of these days, as everyone receives her coffee with a square of fresh baklava placed on the side of the saucer, Em Yousef looks at her daughter with pride and announces, "A few days ago, Mira received a proposal. The groom and his parents visited us and asked for her hand. He is a doctor," she says. "Mira has never met him before, but," she tells them, "he is a good catch."

The other women begin speaking in loud voices. "Mabrouk, Allah ywaf'ek," they say to Mira. Congratulations, may God make you happy! Their words are like party streamers flying. Mira does look happy, I think, for being wanted.

Em Yousef holds her shoulders high and says that they will plan the wedding after Mira graduates from high school in three months. After the wedding, she and the groom will live with his parents. I feel terrified for Mira moving out of her parents' home. Who is this older man who is going to take away my friend, I wonder. I cannot understand why everyone is happy about this news.

The women drink their coffee, and then each one swirls her tiny, delicate cup between her fingertips, swooshing any liquid remnants around to move fine grains of coffee sludge at the bottom up the sides of the cup. The grains make a thin film around the inside walls of the cup that look like hills or mountains or animals or numbers. When she's finished, each woman flips the cup upside down onto its saucer to drain any last bit of liquid that may be remaining in the grains still packed at the bottom. Then they wait for the sludge to dry out while continuing to talk.

During these visits, the energy in the room is quick and strong and chaotic. Everyone speaks at once, and the women jump from one story to another. They talk about who is getting married, giving birth, getting sick, and even dying. It seems that everyone knows each other and is somehow related—"She is my brother's wife's cousin's neighbor's eldest daughter who is married to the engineer," they'll say. The women always manage to keep track of each linkage, but I am always confused about the chain of connections.

When a woman or a man does something deemed unacceptable by family or community standards, the story is repeated over and over. The women share recent news and give their opinions regarding the behavior of others; they seem curious and anxious as they whisper and gasp about tragedies.

When I get sleepy, I get up from the lambskin rug and climb onto the couch next to Tata. I lie down and put my head on her lap. She plays with my hair and starts tapping my shoulder to soothe me to sleep. While everyone is immersed in overlapping conversations and laughter, I doze in and out.

"Ya haram—" what a pity, I hear them say, when a family or husband is abusing a woman. "Aib Alaiha—" shame on her, I hear, when a woman does something deemed inappropriate. "Allah yenajeena," I hear, when a situation is really bad: God protect us from the same situation happening in our own families.

Horrifying stories fill the room. I hear of women who have violated their families' honor and brought so much shame to their families that they are disowned. I hear the women whispering, "Abuha rah yedbaha." I know it is only a saying, but it literally means, "Her father is going to slaughter her," and hearing the words makes me tense. Over and over, I hear about the ways girls are punished for cracks in their vases. The persistent telling reminds girls like Mira and me of the consequences of any crack.

Half asleep and half awake, sometimes I peek at the faces in the room. "Tsk-tsk-tsk," the women repeat in a chorus of disapproving clicks, with their hands on their cheeks and their eyes wide with shock. My chest clenches every time I hear about a woman being threatened for her actions.

When enough time has passed, Em Yousef prepares to read each cup. She flips them over one by one and begins reading the shapes and signs left in the dry coffee grounds at the bottom. "I see an open road," she'll say, or "a tear" or "angry face." The women quiet down to listen as she interprets the shapes to predict their futures. I am too young to drink coffee and too young to have my cup read. This won't happen until I am eighteen, but in my half sleep, I love listening and imagining the possibilities for my own future.

During these weekly visits, laughter, gossip, and stories of shame mingle with beautiful, familiar rituals, turning and swaying like incense smoke. As a result of this strange mix, I am terrified to be anything but perfect.

3　The Graduation Game

The women in my family were not educated beyond high school. Not my mother. Not my aunts. None of these women were permitted to further their educations; they were expected to live in the dark.

Tata wasn't allowed to attend school at all because she was a girl. Instead, she stayed home and helped her mother with the cooking and cleaning. At night, she sat next to her five brothers and listened as they worked on their homework. Her ears were like magnets grabbing every piece of information her brothers spoke aloud. Even without a formal education, Tata was a natural learner.

She loved magazines, but she was not satisfied just looking at the pictures as she flipped through the pages, as her mother, aunts, and cousins did. So she taught herself the shapes and sounds of the alphabet. Her favorite magazine was *Al Mawed*, an Arabic version of *People* magazine filled with the latest Arabic celebrity news. I remember her pointing her index finger to each word and pronouncing it slowly before she moved her finger to the next word. She read her magazines cover to cover; she read anything that she could get her hands on. To her, reading represented independence.

So when I was five years old, she invented a fun game. One day, I heard her call in a deep, loving voice, "Ya Dima, ta'ali." Dima, come here. I put down my dolls and ran to the kitchen, where she spent most of her day cooking. The moment I got there, I saw her standing in her apron next to the worn-out black oven. She was waiting for me, and her round face was shining with a big smile. She motioned me over to her.

Filled with anticipation, I walked toward her. I sensed that she had a big surprise, but I did not realize that I was about to receive the most valuable gift.

As I got closer, she turned to the kitchen table, picked up one of her magazines, carefully rolled it up, and tied it with a red ribbon. I saw her looking at me from the corner of her eye. She leaned down and whispered in my ear, "Today, we are going to play a new game. We are celebrating the day you graduate from college."

She pointed to the rolled magazine, and in a voice filled with love, she said, "I made you a diploma. Sit in this chair and wait for me to announce your name. Then, run to me, and I will hand it to you."

What happens at a graduation? What do you do with a diploma? Why is Tata so happy? I didn't understand anything she said, but all that mattered to me was that I was playing a new game with my favorite person in the world. I nodded with excitement and sat still in the chair.

Tata took four steps back. She stood perfectly straight and raised her head with pride while gripping the diploma as if it were the most valuable object in the world. In a loud, joyful voice, she announced to a large and invisible audience—in our imaginations, thousands of people surrounding us in every direction—"Please join me in congratulating the next graduate, Dima Ghawi."

She gave me a sign to run to her. As I ran, she leaned down

to meet me at eye level. Then she firmly shook my right hand and handed me the diploma. I saw her eyes tear up as she said, "Mabrouk, ana fakhura feeki." Congratulations, I am so proud of you.

We played this game often. Each and every time, I would run to her, and she would present me with my homemade diploma. It was printed on worn and well-read magazine pages hidden inside the tight scroll, but to Tata, it symbolized the desire for a better future, starting with me. I would grip it in one of my small hands. With the other, I would firmly shake Tata's hand and giggle, listening to the imaginary audience cheering for me.

Tata wanted to give me what she and many women in our community had been denied, a formal education. With this simple game, she planted a seed of empowerment in me: I wanted to be the first formally educated woman in our family. Against many odds, but also with some nourishment, the seed grew; it took root in my heart, bloomed in my imagination, and eventually, it brought the fruits of success into my life.

4 Aib

There are rules for being a girl. The rules are not necessarily explicit. We learn them as we go, through trial and error, punishment and consequences. Every time the rules are not followed, it is *aib*: shameful.

When I am seven, Tata visits Egypt and brings home my first dance costume. It is a black dress with a V-neck and hundreds of gold coins stitched on its front and back. I love the shick-shick-shick-shick sounds my dress makes as I turn and twirl everyplace I go. I want to wear it all the time.

I love listening to rhythmic Arabic beats—the way it feels like they are ticking in my bones. I have loved to shake my shoulders and hips to this music for as long as I can remember. When adults ask me what I want to do when I grow up, without hesitation, I answer, "I want to be a dancer."

Every time I say this, my father tilts his head, narrows his eyes, and stares at me. His face stops moving, as if the only thing that remains is the gaze from his eyes to mine. This is a look I remember seeing from the time I was two years old; it is his serious look, his angry look, and the look that frightens me. When I see it, I drop my head, breaking eye contact, and looking down, as I've been taught to do to show my obedience. He makes it clear that dancing is not the kind of profession for which he can feel proud.

By the time I am ten, I've outgrown the dress, and I've stopped saying I want to be a dancer, even though I still love to dance.

The same year, on August 19, 1985, while our family is observing the two-week Catholic period of fasting for the Virgin Mary, we have visitors. My mom has three brothers and a sister: Uncle Qader who lives in Jordan, Uncle Anton who lives in the United States, Auntie Nadia who lives in Canada, and Uncle Zaid who lives in the United States with Uncle Anton. Uncle Anton, Uncle Zaid, and Auntie Nadia all fly in.

My parents send my brother, Waseem; my two-year-old sister, Ruba; and me to stay at my paternal grandmother's house. To celebrate the end of the fasting period, she is making *ma'moul*, traditional shortbread cookies stuffed with a variety of sweet fillings, and this insults my mother.

My brother and I sense our mother's overwhelming sadness, and we know something is going on, because we never stay with *this* grandmother. Tata, we are told, is away on vacation. All of this feels unusual to us.

One month later, I am in Tata's kitchen with my mother. She is wearing a black dress and making French fries, and we're standing next to each other in front of the worn-out oven. Usually, when I am in Tata's kitchen, the radio is playing and the whole room smells of fresh herbs and spices. On this day, there is no music, and I can smell only frying oil that makes the air seem thick.

"Mama, where is Tata?" I keep asking. I have been asking for the entire month, searching for the truth.

Then my mother leans down and, in a shaking voice, she says, "I'm going to tell you something, but you have to be a big girl and stay calm." She looks at me, and tears start dropping down her cheeks. When she sees that I am paying full attention, she wipes her tears and says, "Your grandmother is now in heaven. She had a sudden heart attack and passed away."

When someone dies, it is customary for family members not to perform celebratory acts for a full year, including making *ma'moul*, and women wear only black in that year to express their sadness. Suddenly, I understand why my uncles and auntie had visited, and my mother's anger over my other grandmother making *ma'moul* finally registers.

I stare in silence, numbly watching my mother's hand as she lifts French fries out of the pan with a strainer and places them on a cloth-covered plate to drain the excess oil. I am brokenhearted. I no longer have the fantasy of becoming a professional dancer, the joy of my grandmother's graduation game, or the security of standing next to Tata in her kitchen.

The summer I turn thirteen, my parents enroll my brother and me in a summer camp with our two cousins, Husam and Selma. I am the oldest in the group, the one who is supposed to be a role model.

The camp has many activities, but I am most excited about the *Dabkeh*, a traditional Arabic line dance. I sign up for this activity, and after practicing throughout the summer, the ten-member group of five girls and five boys will perform in front of the other kids as part of the end-of-camp celebration. The celebration includes various events: kids telling jokes, singing songs, performing short plays, and of course, performing our beautiful *Dabkeh* dance. It will be a dream come true for me to perform in front of an audience.

I practice with our camp coach twice a week and diligently

learn the coordinated steps and the patterns—when to clap, when to step forward in the line, when to turn to the beat. I hear the song "Al-Howarra" in my head all day after practices are over. Its beat—quick like flags flapping in strong wind or like a racing pulse—is ingrained in my brain. The day of the performance, I feel ready and happy. I wear blue jeans and a white shirt like the other group members; we agreed ahead of time to match.

Every day around 3:00 p.m., my father picks up my brother, cousins, and me. We wait for him at the curb next to the parking lot. He drops off our cousins at their home, and then he takes my brother and me to our home. My father is rarely early. But on the last day, the day of the performance, he shows up around 1:30 p.m. He arrives just a few minutes after the performance ends. He walks into the camp and finds Waseem and our cousins on the playground with other kids.

"Where is Dima?" he asks.

"She just finished performing *Dabkeh* with a group," the three of them say innocently.

A few minutes later, I walk out of the small camp theater and onto the playground with a sense of accomplishment. I find the four of them standing there. We walk to the car. My father walks in front of us, and my brother, cousins, and I follow him. We start sharing the highlights of our day, but my father is not showing any interest. He is not talking and barely responding to any comments. Something feels strange.

He drops Husam and Selma at their home and waits until the maid opens the door to let them inside. He drives another ten minutes to our home and continues to be silent. He parks the car at the street in front of our home, which is on the third floor of the building. My dad walks up the stairs, rushing past the entryway to Tata's home on the first floor and passing the second floor. When he reaches the third floor, he walks through the big, brown, ugly wooden door that his sister gave to us when we built this home. After my brother and I walk in, my father slams the door.

My mother works during the day to supplement my father's salary, which is not enough to support our family. Typically, we go immediately to the kitchen to eat the dinner that she has prepared for us before leaving for work. But on this day, before even turning toward the kitchen, my dad looks at me with wild, glaring eyes. I freeze in front of him, not understanding why he is mad. But I know that whatever is coming next is going to be painful.

Sometimes, the smallest things make him angry; sometimes, there is no clear reason to justify the screaming that follows his anger. He gets mad often, usually at my brother and my mother. I make sure to behave and follow the rules all the time to avoid this situation.

"How dare you disgrace me," he says. "Did you think that you could do whatever you want to now that you are a teenager?" I still do not understand why he is angry. He yells, "Do you want people to say that MY DAUGHTER dances on a stage? Are you trying to bring me shame?"

He moves around the house, fast and out of control, picking up frames with my pictures. He starts with one on the side table in the living room. In it, I am four years old, smiling, and dressed in a light blue hat with a matching dress that Tata had sewn for me. He throws the picture frame at me. It shatters. One after another, I avoid being hit by the frames and pictures from my early childhood, but I hear them crash against the floor, shattering in all directions. He yells louder, "I am going to teach you a lesson that you will never forget. You better think twice before you do anything that brings me shame again." Then he lunges at me and starts slapping my face, arms, and shoulders while yelling uncontrollably. I want to run away from him, but there is no safe place to go.

All my life, when I begin to cry, he has screamed, "Don't make a sound. Dima, don't make a single sound." On this day, he is in such a state of rage that he doesn't bother to utter these words. But terrified, I am crying exactly the way I've learned to—with tears streaming on the outside and my screams pressed down tight inside of my chest.

I don't know what to do to calm him down. Responding will only make him angrier. Usually in these situations, my mom intervenes, and he starts screaming at her instead. But my mom is at work. After what feels like hours of yelling and hitting, though in reality it might have been a few minutes, he opens the door and walks up the stairs to the rooftop patio, where he spends all of his time after work.

That afternoon is a small taste of the consequences that result from a crack in my vase. With every slap and the glass of every picture frame shattered around me, I learn to obey and stay silent, even if I lose myself. I run to my room, close the door, and cry as I lie on the bed. I want to disappear. I go to sleep, escaping from reality and hoping that when I wake up, the issue will be miraculously gone.

"Wake up, wake up! What have you done?"

I hear my mom's voice, open my eyes, and see her gesturing wildly.

"Your actions caused a big fight," she exclaims, throwing her arms apart in the air. She's still wearing her work clothes. Her eyes are wide, and there is a frown across her face. Her eyebrows are turned inward with frustration; she looks pale and upset.

I realize that after a long day at work, she's come home to my father's anger, and she's figuring out how to calm him down before the situation gets worse.

"Get out of bed," she orders impatiently, "and go to your father to apologize."

"But I did not do anything wrong," I respond. In my mind, I'd been learning a beautiful, traditional dance with other kids my age; but my father had reacted as if I'd been belly dancing on a stage in front of an audience of men, but I knew there was no use in trying to explain.

She looks dissatisfied and somber. She takes a deep breath and says, "The only way this fight is going to be over is if you go to your father, admit that you did something wrong, apologize, and promise him that you will never do anything shameful again." She walks to the door and turns to face me again. "I'll go first to calm him down," she says. Then she adds, "You better follow after me in five minutes."

She walks out of my room and up the staircase to the roof, where I am certain that my father is boiling in his anger.

After a few minutes, I follow. I know in my heart that I did not do anything shameful, and I do not want to apologize. While this is the first time my father has erupted at me so dramatically, it is common for my father to take his anger toward one of us out on my mother. Usually, my mother tries to appease him, doing or saying anything she can think of to end the yelling. Today is one of those times.

I find my brother sitting on the landing between the third and fourth floors. He's listening in as our father screams at our mother. Ruba, who is about four at that time, follows me to the stairs and wants to listen with us. Waseem and I whisper to her at the same time, "Go back inside and close the door." But that does not stop her curiosity, and she keeps opening the door and peeking her head out into the stairwell to listen in. Then our father's anger gets worse. We hear glass shattering, and the three of us look at each other in fear.

"Dima understands that she did something wrong," we hear my mother say in a soft, calm voice. "She regrets it, and she is on her way to apologize to you."

I look at my brother. With my eyes full of tears, I say, "I do not understand what I did wrong. I do not want to apologize." But I know that if I don't apologize, the situation will escalate beyond a level that any of us can manage.

"Dima, come here," my mother calls in a steady voice that masks her nerves. I walk stiffly up the steps and onto the roof.

My dad is smoking apple-flavored tobacco in a hookah. He's holding the pipe in one hand and a cigarette in the other hand. I see the pieces of a crystal glass scattered on the floor. I see the whiskey that once filled the glass making a giant shapeless mark on the wall.

"Baba," I say, "I am sorry." As I hear my words come out, I feel imprisoned by my father's unpredictable, uncontrollable temper. I am chained in fear and have no option but to keep him satisfied. So I ask for his forgiveness and make a promise: "I promise I will never do anything to dishonor or bring you shame, ever again."

5) *The Rules of Honor*

In the Middle East, the day a woman gives birth to her first son is a proud day. When my younger brother was born, my parents named him Waseem, after our paternal grandfather. Following the common tradition, my mother and father took my brother's name. My mother became Em Waseem, "the mother of Waseem." My father became Abu Waseem, "the father of Waseem." This convention celebrates parents for bearing a son.

On the day I was born, when my paternal grandfather learned of my birth, his first words were, "I hope she dies. I want my first grandchild from my oldest son to be a boy." A grandson carries the family name. A granddaughter is a burden to carry—another woman in the family who will need to be protected and controlled to maintain family honor.

Later in life, when I learned about my grandfather's first words after I was born, I shared with my mother how sad his response made me feel. She said, "Don't be upset, Dima. It is not just you. At that time, this was a common saying after a girl was born," as if this was justification for a death wish for my young life.

Looking back, I see that the language itself wrote into existence the rules for respecting men; anyone who learned to speak learned the rules for honoring men. But I didn't learn the rules only from language. I learned them by observing everyone around me, and I watched the rules acted out on television.

We had three channels that broadcast from 10:00 a.m. to 10:00 p.m., and to midnight on weekends. On Fridays, the day the weekends began, Waseem and I watched television for hours. In the morning, an Islamic prayer broadcast for an hour before children's programs began. I remember being six years old and starting the day with cartoons. *Sindibad* was about a hero who traveled the world on adventures and rescued others from distress. We also watched *Mickey Mouse* and *Tom and Jerry*; we loved the mischievous cat chasing after the sneaky little mouse. *Grendizer*, a Japanese cartoon overdubbed in Arabic, was similar to *The Transformers* and *Iron Man*. We lost track of time as we watched these shows.

My brother and I were fascinated by how the television functioned; we imagined that the tiny characters on the screen lived inside the box. At that age, it was difficult to decipher fact from fiction, and the shows we watched left an indelible impression.

In the afternoons, children's programs ended for the day, and Arabic drama series began. We watched Egyptian, Syrian, and Jordanian shows. It seemed that every Egyptian show was a love story that unfolded full of drama and heartbreak. Meddling families disrupted marriages; lovers separated under the pressure of familial conflicts; finally, the lovers reunited against all odds. In these shows, in the name of *Biet at Ta'ah*—the Sharia law that is not actually mentioned in the Quran, but that is enforced in the court system—I watched husbands drag their wives back home after they'd tried to leave bad marriages. The men called the police, who enforced the law, which protects a man's right to refuse a divorce by forcing wives back to the husbands even if the wives were physically abused. I stayed glued to these shows.

Syrian films often referenced an ancient saying that stayed with me, "Slaughter the cat on the wedding night." In episodes that featured weddings, fathers gave this advice to sons. The saying was connected to a legend. Long ago, on his wedding night, a man would slaughter a cat in front of his new bride to show her that he was in control, and that she must fear and obey him. Watching these movies, I learned early that men dominate their wives from the beginning of a marriage; otherwise, they are considered weak.

My father used to join us in front of the television after the children's programs ended. Together, we watched Bedouin films that are similar to American westerns. Like cowboys staking claim in the Wild West, nomadic Bedouin tribes, who are revered as the purest representatives of Arab culture, lived in tents and herded animals in harsh desert circumstances; above all, they preserved strict codes of honor. The Bedouins were a brute force, and in the final scenes of these films, it was not uncommon for the Bedouins to kill someone. The victim was usually a woman who had disobeyed or disrupted the family order. She was executed to preserve the family honor.

Bedouin men were supposed to be heroes restoring order to their families and community, but my heart raced as I watched the offending woman being killed. There was always a bolt of fear running through my body. As the woman on the screen was dying, her tears and blood streamed together; her regret was always evident too late. My father, gripped by tension, watched the ending like a spectator in an arena; he was always relieved by the final outcome.

"She deserves it!" he used to proclaim. "Blood erases shame and brings lost honor back to the family." He spoke these words so many times, over so many years, and over so many movies. I was reminded, always, that the victim deserved to be killed for sacrificing her tribe's good name, for sacrificing the tribe's honor.

My brother, sister, and I used to watch television in Tata's sunroom, on the first floor of our building. The room had a white limestone wall on one side and, on the other side, a wall of windows that looked out over the front yard toward the street. The television was a big piece of wooden furniture. Set on top of it, there was a framed picture of my mom's youngest brother, Uncle Zaid, in Venice surrounded by a crowd of more than fifty pigeons. This picture fascinated me because the pigeons seemed still and unafraid, instead of ready to fly away. Beneath the television, there was a VCR on a shelf. On either side of the screen, Tata kept potted plants. Two bamboo chairs faced the screen, and we either sat in the chairs or lay on our stomachs on the floor, propped up on our elbows with our chins in our hands.

"Dima, Waseem," my grandmother always instructed, "move away from the television; it will damage your eyes."

We would scoot back until she wasn't paying attention or until we got too lost in the shows to notice that we'd moved closer again.

I learned the many expectations for women and the many privileges men were entitled to from hours sitting in front of the television. I learned, for example, that a bride should have parents who are respected in the community. The bride's mother should not have a reputation for being too demanding or for influencing her daughter too much. I learned that a wife must satisfy her husband's needs and desires. I learned from television, and I saw in my own home, that most traditional men did not clean or cook or help raise the children. I learned that a man could "explore" before he got married; he could sleep around. When it came time for a wedding, he expected to marry a virgin, someone younger, who was naïve about the world.

While watching these movies, Tata used to say, "She's like a kitten, brand new to this world, with her eyes still closed." Commenting on the young heroine's inexperience and naïveté was always a compliment. If the hero discovered his bride was not a virgin, he could demonstrate his power and regain his honor by leaving her on the wedding night. I learned that a man's word was the final word, and he should never show soft emotions; they displayed weakness. "Hada tartoor," the older women would say—he's a sissy.

I never met a woman in real life who'd been forced to go back to her abusive husband, dragged by police, because of *Biet at Ta'ah*, though somewhere, this may have happened. I never met a family in which a disobedient woman had been killed for the sake of restoring family honor. Watching television gave me a picture at an early age that, whether true or false, became embedded as reality in my psyche and in the psyches of many boys and girls. Men earned respect by the mere act of being born, but they learned quickly that it was up to them to maintain that honor. Women learned quickly to submit to men's honor.

Just as I thought cartoon characters were tiny beings that lived behind the screen and inside the television box, whether fact or fiction, I believed the messages and stories that played out on the screen in the adult programs. Subjecting women to fear, injustice, and inequality as a means to maintain the rule of order for honoring men was a normalized way of thinking; it was an indisputable fact of life.

6 The Men I Remember

The men I remember had thick mustaches or neatly trimmed beards. Their hair was naturally black. Most had round bellies with belts buckled snugly underneath; the bellies got bigger as the men got older.

They dressed in linen pants and shirts, but they were very rarely casual, except for Uncle Zaid, who had studied and worked in the United States before returning to Jordan and who always wore shorts at home.

They acted wealthy, even if they were not. This was another way for them to show their manhood. My father always repeated what his father used to say: "I am willing to borrow money, even if I am poor, in order to treat any guests to the best food and hospitality." Was he a generous man? Was he boastful? Was he only repeating a pattern he had learned? It's possible that all of these are true.

The men I remember looked serious and responsible. They had families, children, cars, and jobs. At gatherings, they sat next to each other on couches and chairs while their wives gathered in the kitchen. The women shared the latest news with one another and circled back and forth out to the dining room or guest room or rooftop patio to serve the men trays full of food.

When the talks got lively, the men told the children and young adults to go to another room so they could share dirty jokes and laugh loudly. The men also discussed politics and the latest wars. If they disagreed with each other, their voices grew louder, and they interrupted one another like car horns, or they cut each other off like traffic whizzing on a freeway at night. I never saw them physically fight, but many times I saw that a fight was close, until another man stepped in and ended the argument.

The men I remember—my father, my uncles, family friends, and acquaintances—were passionate. Loud, passionate laughter could quickly become loud, passionate anger. I learned early, watching my father and watching all of the men, to accept that passion was a line between two distinct sides that could be crossed without warning.

My father's erratic behavior is what I most remember. His anger was unpredictable, especially within the walls of our home. When I was growing up, the excuse was always, "Oh, he's a man. He's angry," or else, "This is *your* fault. What have you done to make him angry?" For him, and for all of the men whom I saw act the way he did, women were always offering excuses. There were blame, guilt, and justification.

Uncle Anton, my mother's older brother, was the exception; he was a different kind of man from her oldest and youngest brothers and from my father and his one brother. Uncle Anton had already moved to the United States when I was born, but he visited us in Jordan on four different occasions—once when I was about six, once for Tata's funeral, once when I was sixteen, and finally, for my wedding.

During that first visit, I remember watching him as he would quietly sit and close his eyes. He called it his "meditation time." It was strange to my brother and me. We would sneak into the room where he was meditating, watch him, and try to hold ourselves back from bursting out laughing. We had never seen any-one sitting in silence in a room. We were used to people being loud—laughing loudly, screaming loudly, and expressing them-selves without controlling their emotions.

Uncle Anton explained to us that it is important to give our brain a break and not allow our monkey thoughts to take over. He invited us to meditate with him and explained that we needed to focus on our breath instead of our thoughts. I knew that it would be boring, and it was, but I would sit next to him, with my legs crossed and my eyes closed, trying to follow his lead.

No one in my family read regularly except for magazines. My father read once in a while, if it was required for his work. But Uncle Anton always had books with him on his visits, and he read for pleasure and his own curiosity. He always seemed to have deep knowledge about many different topics. He read every night before he went to sleep, and he shared his knowledge with my brother and me. It was strange to see him reading books, and it was even stranger to have this adult sharing information from these books with us children.

With each visit, and with phone calls and letters in between, Uncle Anton left a lasting impression.

7 Truth and Beauty

I left Jordan when I was twenty. I imagine and hope that a lot has changed over time. Yet I cannot deny my experience of men and women when I was a young girl—the understood rules and common behaviors, the generational restrictions and perpetuated expectations. Together, these painted the picture I saw when I opened my eyes to my world each day. Is my story "the norm"? My story *is* the norm, and, it is also *not* the norm.

When I was fourteen or fifteen, I knew a girl named Hala. She was my age, and her purpose in life as a young adolescent was to wake up and clean the house each day and to cook meals for her parents and brothers. By 1:00 p.m., she showered and dressed to look her best. She waited anxiously for guests to visit, hoping that one of the neighbors or family friends would know of a bachelor son, consider Hala as a potential wife and as an obedient daughter-in-law, and then convince the son to offer Hala a marriage proposal. Her parents kept her naïve, uneducated, and with no experiences or identity of her own. She was taught not to question the norm and to follow traditions and rules. Her main desire in life was to get married, as if marriage was the only way to a better life, and her main purpose was to serve everyone around her without complaint.

Another girl, Zahra, was one of the top students in our high school class. She was a star in physics, and she was also quiet and calm. As soon as she passed the *Tawjihi*, a competitive Jordanian high school exam, her family married her off. They told her that to meet her husband ahead of time would be *aib*—that she must trust that her father had arranged a marriage to the right man for her. She met her husband for the first time on the day of their wedding.

On the other hand, my friend Farah's parents were open-minded and modern. They encouraged Farah to apply for university overseas. She got a scholarship and went to Harvard to study law. She met her husband outside the traditional family introductions; she is now a wife and mother, and yet, she's also a successful attorney.

My best friend Bana's parents sent her to study in Lebanon. Afterward, she moved to England to earn her master's degree. Because of her worldly experiences and Western way of thinking, Bana was not allowed to come to our home; I was forbidden to talk to her. My father could not bear the fact that Bana's father permitted her to experience life and to pursue her dreams; he believed that she was a bad influence on me.

So, I knew the fourteen-year-old girl waiting for a husband, and within five kilometers, I knew the girl whose father sent her to Harvard Law School. Both are true, because truth exists on a spectrum.

I was an average Middle Eastern woman of my generation. I was allowed to go to school, but I was expected not to get *too* educated or independent. In my family's eyes, I was still destined to get married and have children early in life. My education would be a status symbol, a prestigious accomplishment to make me more attractive as the right kind of wife for the right kind of husband. I'd be educated, but I'd stay in my box, within my limits. I'd be a trophy. I was allowed to meet my husband before marriage, but I was expected to follow the traditions of showing no intimacy or closeness once we were engaged. These things put me in the middle of the spectrum.

Just as truth for women in the Middle East exists on a spectrum, other cultural realities exist on a full spectrum. There are parts of the culture I grew up with that were oppressive, abusive, and ugly. There are also many parts of my upbringing that are beautiful and comforting.

I felt that God's presence was around me at all times; God was in every sight and sound in Amman. Throughout spring and summer, I watched sheep crossing the street—large flocks walked together, guided by a shepherd who took them from one area of fresh green grass to another. Traffic came to a halt; cars idled and waited for the sheep and their shepherd to cross. I used to look down on this scene from our rooftop patio and observe the fluffy white bodies drift en masse slowly across the city street. It was as if I were watching from heaven, looking down on clouds.

After Christmas, Ramadan, Easter, and *Eid Al Adha*, the Islamic holy day that honors Abraham's devotion and willingness to sacrifice his son at God's command, schools and businesses shut down for three days while families visited each other's homes in a steady stream. Muslim families knocked on the doors of Christian families. Christian families knocked on the doors of Muslim families. The sense of community and celebration was shared and all encompassing.

Sons and daughters dressed in new clothes. Fathers and sons went out, meeting with friends and family members. Mothers and daughters stayed home, greeting the guests and serving them trays of homemade treats. For Christmas, we baked three types of *ma'moul* cookies: stuffed with dates, pistachios, or walnuts. During Easter, my mother put out a huge basket of dyed eggs and a huge basket of egg-shaped chocolates decorated with blue, pink, and white Jordan almonds. Our guests visited with us for fifteen or twenty minutes—more often than not, multiple families arrived at one time. We caught up on the news in their lives, and after they left, we waited eagerly for the next group of visitors to arrive. These were warm, informal holiday open houses. Every knock on the door was a welcomed knock. Every house in the city buzzed with festivity.

During the Muslim holy month of Ramadan, the *Musaher* walks through the streets beating his decorated *Tabbel* drum and singing. The *Musaher*'s job is to wake sleepers for the *Suhoor*, the predawn meal Muslims eat before fasting for the day. Though my family was Christian, each year I looked forward to hearing the deep beat, "tum-ta-Tum-Tum," reverberate through the air in every direction, followed by the *Musaher* singing.

"Wake up, fasters, and praise Allah! Welcome Ramadan, the month of forgiveness!" The *Musaher* called out these words and followed them with three deep, even beats on his drum, before continuing to sing. His chant and drum seemed to echo in the otherwise dark silence.

I loved waking to the sound of his drum and his beautiful voice. I used to hear the beat from a street far away. As the intensity of the sound increased, I knew he was getting closer. Sometimes, I peeked into the darkness from the window next to my bed, trying to get a glimpse of this ancient tradition as the *Musaher* moved past our home and then onto the next. As the last bit of the rhythm faded into the air, I rolled to the other side of my bed, hoping to return to dreaming.

Throughout the years, I also heard the *Athan*, the Islamic call to prayer, recited five times a day. It played through a loudspeaker from all the mosques and filtered into homes through open windows. The fifth and last one of each day reminded people that it was time to enter into their houses and end the day in worship.

"*Allaaaaaaaaaaaaaahu* Akbar" sang through the speaker like an unending silk scarf stretching and flowing down from the heavens. "Allahu Akbar," God is great, the *Athan* called out.

Islamic calls to prayer are as woven into my memory as the Christian traditions my family practiced. All of these traditions are familiar, comforting, glimmering jewels that I can still see and hear. It is precisely my clear, visceral memory of such beauty, especially beauty so deeply intertwined with God, that makes it hard for me to rectify the heartbreaking truths of my upbringing. Yet I have to believe that out of accepting and declaring the harsh truths of my life, my future and the futures of generations to come will be impacted—more beauty will grow, where once there was anguish.

8   *An Educated Woman*

It was July 1989 during a large gathering on our rooftop patio. I was fourteen, no longer a child but not yet an adult. My mother, aunt, and I had been cooking for the last week, preparing the ingredients and baking the pastries, then freezing them. The hour before the party, we heated everything and filled the buffet table with homemade cheese, kabobs, spinach pies, freshly mixed tabbouleh, hummus, baba ghanouj, dark green stuffed grape leaves, stuffed zucchini, and broiled chicken pieces set over light brown freekeh grains and placed on a big round silver dish garnished with toasted pine nuts and almonds.

We had over fifty guests, all eating, laughing, and smoking hookahs. Most of my close female relatives and friends were rushing to pour food in serving dishes, cleaning the side tables of empty plates and glasses, or washing dishes. Like them, I was going up and down the stairs, bringing food from our kitchen up to the roof; clearing empty plates from the tables and carrying them back to the kitchen; or asking the adults if they needed another whiskey, beer, Pepsi-Cola, or a refill of Arak, a fermented anise alcohol.

Other women were standing in groups, looking around and commenting on other guests or mutual acquaintances—whispering just above the Arabic music about their outfits and the latest fashions, whose relationships were working or not, news of people getting married or engaged, potential marriage matches, rumors of women getting pregnant, or daughters causing trouble at home—the kinds of stories people weren't supposed to share too openly or too loudly. These women were the role models I was most accustomed to.

In the chaos of serving food and drinks while groups of adults talked and children ran around, danced to music, or played hide-and-seek, a middle-aged woman who was standing next to the buffet table caught my eye. She was not gossiping or reacting to this kind of frivolous commentary. Instead, she was discussing politics, giving her opinions about the last US election, the resulting global-economic implications of the Iran-Iraq War that had ended a year earlier, and other worldly subjects. I observed her elegant gestures and how smoothly she spoke to both women and men about intellectual matters, how she listened with concentration, nodding her head slightly while maintaining eye contact with the people in her group. I was completely captivated by this woman's unique style and confidence. Her composure was riveting.

As my mother's sister, Auntie Nadia, rearranged the dishes on the table to make space for fresh plates that she had brought up from the kitchen, she noticed that I was staring at the stranger. Watching me watch the woman, Auntie Nadia accidentally knocked over a glass of water that was on the edge of the table. It dropped on the floor and shattered, and the guests turned their heads to look at the commotion. One by one, they smiled and shouted, "Inkasar il shar," the traditional saying when someone breaks a glass by mistake—the evil just got shattered!

Someone rushed to bring Auntie Nadia a towel, and she began cleaning the spill. After she stood, holding the wet towel filled with sharp glass pieces, she leaned in to me and whispered, "Dima, maybe one day you will get educated too, and you will be like her."

I learned that the woman's name was Amal, "hope" in Arabic. She had a master's degree in business from the United States. She worked with Uncle Zaid at the Marriott in Jordan and specialized in sales and hospitality. I heard later from my uncle that she was one of the most respected women in his office. She had a leadership role; she even had a higher status than my uncle's. Between running up and down the stairs, I continued to observe her and listened closely to catch anything she said.

I was a quiet, obedient student and daughter; I avoided bold behavior. I did not have a powerful, educated female role model, but that night, I unexpectedly found one in a total stranger whom I was too shy to even exchange words with. Instead, for less than three hours, I studied her diligently, and then I never saw her again.

But some generational evil did get shattered that night, bringing a ray of hope into my sight. Amal's impression ignited a fire in me. I wanted to look, talk, move, walk, and sound like her. The dream of this possibility, of being like Amal, felt exhilarating in the face of expectations that felt debilitating.

It was a confusing time; the messages I grew up with were conflicting. My parents had insisted that I should always come home with perfect grades; nothing less would have been acceptable. They wanted me to study day and night throughout high school to get competitive grades so I would be accepted to the University of Jordan, the only public-accredited university in Amman at the time. I was raised to believe that my education was paramount.

On the other hand, they also held traditional values; they impressed upon me the importance of getting married while I was still young and providing my husband with healthy children soon after, with the idea that I would become a caretaker, the ideal wife and mother. For them, as long as I held my university diploma, it didn't matter what I did with it. The diploma itself would be a point of family pride and a status symbol to help me attract a more prestigious husband.

I remember being an ambitious sixteen-year-old student. That year, I learned to graph x- and y-axes and how to use them to calculate slope in my math class. When the school year ended, Uncle Anton came for a visit. I had just finished my final exams, and I was excited to show off my knowledge to him. The information was still fresh in my head.

I was sitting next to him on the couch in Tata's home, where my maternal grandfather now lived alone. I knew Uncle Anton was an economist, and I proudly mentioned that I knew how to calculate a slope.

"Working with slopes is one of the topics I teach my students at the university," he told me. "We use slopes to study trends in economics. Dima, do you enjoy math?" he asked.

I nodded and told him that I did. I felt pleased that he was curious about my interests and that we had something in common.

"Why don't you get your books and show me what you've learned?" he suggested. We sat looking at math problems for over an hour, going through the pages as he read my notes on the sides and discussed the information, showing me alternative ways to solve the problems. Then he asked, "Dima, what do you want to study in college?"

"Baba wants me to get my bachelor's degree in pharmacy,"

I answered automatically. "He says it will give me flexibility to have reasonable work hours, so when I get married, my job won't demand too much of my attention. I'll have enough time to take care of my family."

"Pharmacy is a good degree; it leads to a good profession," he said. Then he added, "You are a smart girl, so you can explore a lot of options. And you don't have to stop at your bachelor's if you don't want to." He began telling me about his degrees. I was amazed to learn that he had a bachelor's, a master's, and a PhD. Not only that, but his American wife, Auntie Annette, had her bachelor's and two master's degrees. He told me, "She is thinking about pursuing her PhD as well. So," he asked again, "what do you want to study?"

I knew I wanted to achieve the dream Tata had held for me—to become the first educated woman in our family, but at the time, I didn't have a specific ambition beyond receiving my diploma. Yet Uncle Anton, who was used to working with eighteen- and nineteen-year-olds in the States, treated me and spoke to me as if I were one of his American students—as if my personal ambitions and interests mattered beyond making me a prestigious, marketable bride. It was a completely foreign experience.

"I don't know," I said. I remembered the advice my mom's eldest brother had given me. "Uncle Qader is encouraging me to enroll in secretarial school. He told me, 'Your future priority should be your husband and your children. Look at my assistant,' he explained to me one time. 'She can leave work early, get her kids from school, and still be home to have dinner ready and on the table when her husband gets home.'"

Uncle Anton laughed and groaned, at once. "Oh, no!" he exclaimed. He turned his entire body away from me, throwing his hands over his temples, as he shook his head in disbelief. He turned back to face me, and said, "Listen, Dima. A college degree gives a woman freedom. It arms her with the power to choose her life and to protect herself." He leaned in: "You need to get educated. Don't agree to get married before you have a degree in your hand."

He looked at me thoughtfully and added, "I used to watch my uncles and aunties eager to marry off their daughters. So many of my female cousins were married to the first man who approached their parents with a proposal. They got married young, and they didn't have a chance to get a degree or any marketable skills." He paused and his face saddened. He went on, "Some of them ended up with much older, abusive men."

I listened to him and didn't say much. But I knew what he was talking about; I had observed these things as well. But I had just never questioned the situation; I had always thought of this as a normal occurrence instead of the result of a series of deliberate decisions elders made for their children.

Uncle Anton continued, "They end up cooking and cleaning all day, with no hope. They are abused, but they can't survive on their own, and their parents would not take them back if they tried to leave the marriages. It is wrong, so wrong. Don't allow the same tragedy to happen to you as what I've seen with my cousins—and this, by the way, is also the case with your mother."

I sat staring at him and trying to process the information. It was the first time I had ever had a deep conversation about my education and my future as a woman, and it was the first time anyone had admitted that they could see my mother's misery. Uncle Anton spoke to me as if I were an adult. I liked that feeling, but he was offering a new way to look at the world, and I could only take it all in quietly.

"Al'ilmu noor," he said. Knowledge is light. He looked at me and paused.

I had seen these words written hundreds of times in Arabic

calligraphy that unfurled like a dancing ribbon; until then, the words had always been just a decoration—an inspirational saying hanging on a wall.

Uncle Anton smiled at me in a gentle way, and he asked, "Do you understand what I'm telling you?"

I nodded. I understood. I had seen my father abuse my mother. I had seen her tears and depression, but no one had ever spoken to me frankly about her situation or how mine could be different.

Uncle Anton encouraged me to finish my degree before getting married and to specialize in anything I wanted to. It seemed that there were no limits to education in his world, for men *and* for women. I trusted his experience, but I had trouble believing it could be true for me. I wanted to believe that I could also live in the world he spoke about, but I wasn't sure I could. The mixed messages battled in my brain.

Still, I looked up at him and finally said, "I understand, Uncle."

"Good," he said, and he asked one last time, "Now . . . tell me, what would you like to study?"

I was thinking about this question when, suddenly, his face lit up. "Dima! I just saw your grandmother's face in yours when I looked at you." Without taking a breath between sentences, he said, "You have her round face and her dark, beautiful eyes."

I held his gaze. It was an emotional moment for both of us. I wondered if her spirit was there, surrounding us and encouraging him to teach me more and more, to water the seed that she had planted a decade before.

Tata planted the seed for graduation. The stranger at the party showed me it was possible. But Uncle Anton watered the seed Tata had planted; he nurtured the dream of a path for education that was not limited to just one degree or to marriage and family. Even though I was flattered and even encouraged by my uncle's belief in me, that dream stayed dormant at first.

9 Footsteps in the Snow

The beautiful memories of my father come in rare, short flashes, like the strikes of matches that burn out quickly. Then they are gone. This is one of them.

I am studying for the *Tawjihi*. In the weeks leading up to the exam, my father sets his alarm clock for early in the morning. He walks to my bedroom to wake me at four o'clock every morning so I can study for two hours before I leave for school. He juices carrots and boils Turkish coffee for me, and sometimes, he sits at the kitchen table chatting with me until I am fully awake. Every so often, he checks in to make sure I am still awake and to see if I need anything.

After school, I study again at the kitchen table. He forbids my brother and sister to walk into the kitchen, even for a glass of water. He does not want them to disturb my concentration. When I'm frustrated or anxious, he says, "Dima, if it was easy, everyone would do it." He believes that I am smart, that I have the ability to excel. And he is right—the exam isn't easy, but I do very well. A father believes in his daughter.

Another flash: Dalal lives with her parents on the first floor of a three-story building next door to our home. She's in her late thirties and teaches chemistry. In the afternoons, I walk to her house to be tutored.

One day, there's a snowstorm. Over a foot and a half of snow is on the ground. It rarely snows in Amman, so when it does, the city shuts down and no one goes to work or school. If I do well on the *Tawjihi*, I'll qualify to apply to the University of Jordan. But I'm anxious about the chemistry portion of the exam. I don't want to cancel my session with Dalal.

My dad and I bundle up in our coats. I carry my heavy books and notebook in my bag. We don't have proper snow boots. Outside, the city is silent and still, like a snow globe on display, chalk-white buildings beneath a blanket of white snow.

Baba walks in front of me, making giant footsteps in the snow, pressing hard with each step and paving a path for me to follow in. "Step in my tracks," he tells me.

I jump from one deep, oversized footstep to the next. When we arrive, his feet are cold and wet, and mine are practically dry. My father walking his daughter through the snow.

10 ⟩ *Destiny Written on the Forehead*

I attended a private Christian girls' school, which was a conservative and sheltered environment. I fantasized about the freedom I would have once I made it to the university. I imagined that I would be able to meet men and women outside my family's supervision for the first time in my life. I could practice building friendships in my own way. I thought that I may even meet a man who would be interested in me, and we'd have a fairy-tale romance.

But when I enrolled at the University of Jordan, my father did not want me to talk to men. On the first day, before I walked out the door, he told me, "I'm sending you to school, and I'm trusting you. *Ya walek*—if you dare to speak to men and I find out, know that it will be the end. You'll stay home, and I'll find someone to marry you." Then he reminded me that my curfew was 4:00 p.m. My classes ended at 3:00 p.m., and I had one hour to get back home afterward. He said, "Do you hear me—four o'clock. Not a minute later."

In spring of 1994, when I was still eighteen and in my second semester of college, Nader, a popular student who was in the School of Business, began telling me how much he liked me and asking me to date him. I resisted his requests at first, but then I began to skip classes to make time to talk with him. We spent about two months walking together or sitting on a bench and having long conversations. It was a brief, secret friendship. When the semester ended, he traveled to the United States for the summer, and I longed for his companionship.

That summer, I went to Em Simone's house with my mother to have my fortune read from coffee grounds for the first time. Em Simone was one of Tata's friends, and for as long as I could remember, once a month, my mother visited her to have her cup read.

It was one of the few acts my mother took comfort in. She was seeking messages of hope, signs of something positive to look forward to, or warnings about situations she needed to prepare for ahead of time—especially related to my father's unpredictable temper and his family that always caused conflict in their marriage. She was stuck in an unhealthy marriage, trying to survive day by day, and she believed, like everyone else, that she did not have the power to change her destiny.

Em Simone's home was a twenty-minute walk from our home. She was known to gossip, and her home was always filled with clutter. Members of the community, both women and men, disregarded these flaws and were always nice to her, because she was known for giving accurate fortunes.

My mother and I would carefully listen to everything Em Simone said—predictions about future gatherings, individuals my mother needed to be careful in dealing with, experiences that were coming her way at work and in our family—and immediately we would try to link her interpretations to whatever was happening in our lives. Depending on her reading, my mother walked back to our home with either a feeling of concern or a sense of hope.

I was curious about whether she would read anything related to Nader. At the same time, I left with a mix of disappointment, yet relief that he never came up in front of my mother.

When summer was ending, Nader returned to Amman. We met in secret at the university, and I was ecstatic to see him again. Sitting beside him on a bench, with butterflies in my stomach, I listened as he told me about his adventures in America. Then, he began telling me about the physical relationships he'd had with women there. My stomach, at first filled with excited nerves, sank. Though we hadn't been in a committed relationship, or even in a physical relationship, I felt sick, hurt, and angry. It felt like I had been cheated on.

Not long after, while I was still working through these feelings, Nader started asking me to become intimate with him. He wanted more than conversation and occasional kisses. I knew that if I took what was a fairly innocent friendship any further, it would destroy my family and create an unforgivable and irreparable crack in my vase. I refused, and he immediately distanced himself from me. He stopped responding to my calls.

I felt heartbroken and wondered if anyone would ever admire me the way it felt like Nader had at the beginning. I was overwhelmed with sadness and couldn't hide my emotions. It felt like I'd been through a breakup. I had to tell my mother.

We were sitting next to each other on my bed, and I told her, "I have something bad that I have to share with you. Please promise that you will not be upset."

"You can tell me anything," she said. "We are more than a mother and a daughter; we are friends."

Then, I told her about Nader with a mixture of words and sobs. She listened without interruption and forced herself to contain her shock and to seem understanding. When I finished telling her what happened, she let out a deep breath.

She was relieved to know the relationship was over. She reminded me of the importance of my pure reputation and said, "Dima, don't share this experience with anyone."

Em Simone didn't share any revealing or life-changing messages about my life until November 1994, several months after I'd ended things with Nader. I remember sitting next to my mother on Em Simone's brown couch and watching Em Simone as she was sitting in a matching chair to our right. The dark brown coffee table in front of us had a tray placed on top of a white, handmade crocheted cover. The tray held a copper pot, half filled with freshly boiled steaming Turkish coffee, a plate with *ma'moul* cookies, and one coffee cup, my mother's, turned upside down onto its saucer to dry out the coffee grounds.

As soon as I finished drinking my coffee, I started swirling the remaining liquid in my cup, tilting it up and peering in to make sure the liquid and grounds were coating the sides of the cup. Then I flipped it upside down onto its saucer and placed it on the tray next to my mother's cup. Once the cups were dry, Em Simone lifted each cup and began to read our fortunes from the shapes left in the dried coffee grounds. She started with mine.

"Shu'feelna shu maktoub," my mother said. Tell us what is written in the grounds.

Em Simone put on her reading glasses and said, "Inshallah khair," hopefully all good. Then she examined the cup, turning it around and searching for signs. "I see a tall woman with her son planning a visit to your home," she finally said. "I see two rings. A marriage proposal will result from that visit." She paused and squinted at the bottom of the cup, and added, "And I see a move across water."

My mother and I looked at each other. We could not imagine who this tall woman or her son could be.

When I was growing up, Tata and many of my elders used to say, "It is written on the forehead." They believed that the story of our lives is predetermined before we are even born. Some people are lucky to be granted great lives, while others, like my mother, are given a difficult destiny. The elders believed and taught that nothing could be done to change the destiny that was written on the forehead. Like so much else, destiny was something we needed to accept and live with, without trying to change its course.

Still, Em Simone's reading did not line up with my life at that moment, so I dismissed her prediction. But less than a month after the visit with Em Simone, my parents got a phone call from my father's distant cousin, Dawoud Haddad, and his wife, Kasma, who was taller than the average women in our community. They called to ask if they could come for a Christmas visit. Amo Dawoud said, "Kasma and I are planning to bring our son with us. It is about time for the new generation of Haddad and Ghawi cousins to meet each other."

PART TWO
Cracks

11 Tests of Worth

In the small community where I grew up, as a newborn girl opens her eyes to the first beam of light, her family welcomes her to the world with gifts of tiny pieces of shiny yellow-gold jewelry. The size of these gifts of gold increases slightly with each new candle on her birthday cakes.

On her wedding day, she receives a bounty of earrings, necklaces, and rings from her family, husband, and in-laws. These gold gifts are more than beautiful treasures; they represent her worth and status in the community. I was one of these women. I was raised to believe that my worth was directly linked to the gold standard of how much of this prestigious metal I possessed.

By my second year at the University of Jordan, my parents no longer cared about my grades; they only wanted me to do well enough to earn a degree. I internalized their attitudes. After working intensely during high school, I was no longer motivated to be the best in the class. I absolutely wanted to be the first formally educated woman in our family, but, like my parents, I believed my degree would amount to a prestigious piece of paper. I understood that my first priority after graduating would be to fulfill their expectation to get married young, have children soon after, and raise them the way that I had been raised.

Uncle Anton's encouragement over the years about professional aspirations had been flattering, but I wasn't yet motivated to challenge the norm; to do so seemed impossible.

Not long before Amo Dawoud and Amto Kasma called my parents, my mother and father had an explosive fight. My father was volatile. He shouted vulgarities into the air and at my mother. He slammed doors and broke plates and glasses, while my seventeen-year-old brother, my eleven-year-old sister, and I listened through the walls from the safety of our closed bedrooms. This was such a common occurrence: my father raged at my mother, and she would work to calm him down, doing or saying whatever she needed to in order to convince him that she was sorry for the perceived indiscretion—just as she'd asked me to do on the rooftop that year after summer camp ended.

However, there was something unusual about this particular fight. After it ended, my mother came into my room. She was in tears. She did not explain what caused the fight. She did not complain about her circumstances. She did not make excuses for my father.

She simply said, "Dima, listen to me—if you get a proposal from a good man, accept it and leave this house." Her voice was steady and detached. As if she was remembering Nader, she added, "Even if I disapprove and try to convince you otherwise in the moment, even if the situation is not perfect, get married and leave. You deserve a better life."

Malek Haddad was the most eligible bachelor in our small, Christian community in Amman. While our family was Catholic, and his family was Anglican, what was most important to my parents was that we were part of the same religion. Beyond this, his parents had an impeccable reputation. Amo Dawoud was a respected jeweler who owned a store in the gold market in downtown Amman, and Amto Kasma represented the perfect Middle Eastern woman in our community: she was always well dressed and well spoken. I'd heard community members compliment, "Kasma bit'oom bil wajeb—" that she was a woman who showed the proper respect in every public situation. She visited the ill, attended every funeral, chose the right gifts for newlyweds and for newborns, and took a gift with her every time she visited someone's home. She was well liked and charismatic. There were no cracks in her vase.

Their son Malek had been educated in the United States, which was usually an indication of being more worldly and Western-minded than the average Middle Eastern man. He had also achieved success at a relatively young age. He had partnered with his elder brother and started a jewelry manufacturing company that designed, created, and supplied their precious pieces to other jewelers to display and sell in their shops. At twenty-nine, ten years senior to me, his parents bragged about him and his brother having a million dollars in their business account. In addition to all of this, his family had plans to expand their business with a move to the United States.

So when my parents heard the knock on our door on the evening of December 18, 1994, they began eagerly straightening their clothes and smoothing their hair as they rushed to let our visitors into the house.

I hid behind my bedroom door, peeking through the crack, apprehensive about this introduction. I could only see Malek's back, in an impressive red, yellow, and navy blue striped dress shirt with well-ironed beige pants. I didn't want to go out to greet him.

My mother rushed to my room. She knocked on my door and, without waiting for it to open, said, "Dima, aren't you ready?" My parents had insisted that I skip my afternoon classes that day to come home early, take a nap, and then take my time to get ready. They wanted me to look naturally relaxed and effortlessly beautiful for our guests. That afternoon, my mother told me that several years earlier, when she had first met Malek, she had prayed to the Virgin Mary that he would marry me. Now her dreams might come true. "You must come out," she insisted.

"No. I won't," I said. I wanted a love story. I wanted to wake up each morning feeling admired by my future husband. I had no reason to believe that a man my family arranged to introduce me to could possibly adore me.

"It's impolite. Our guests are expecting to see you," my mother said in a lower voice, so our guests would not hear. Frustrated, she continued, "If you don't come out, I'm going to get your father, and he will make you come out."

"I really don't want to meet him," I said. In addition to resisting this introduction, I did not feel ready for marriage. I knew that eventually I would get married, but I was hoping to graduate and have an opportunity to choose someone with whom I was compatible.

When my dad came to my room, it took only a firm look and a few words, "Out, right now." With that, I complied.

Dreading the moment more with each step, I walked to the guest room to meet this man for the first time. When I saw him, I was thunderstruck: he was tall, fit, handsome, and immediately charming. He had a magnetic energy, and in his presence, I became perceivably awkward. I sensed the warm blood rushing to my face, causing me to blush. When I shook Malek's hand, I felt my world change. I felt an instant and absolute connection. I felt as if I were going to melt in his handshake.

As I shook Amo Dawoud's hand and said hello to Amto Kasma, I could see from the corner of my eye that Malek was watching my every move. We all sat down around the coffee table. His parents were seated beside each other on the couch, with a window behind them and the long edge of the table in front of them. My parents were across from them on a loveseat, with the kitchen door behind them. Malek and I were sitting in chairs at the opposite ends of the table, face-to-face, but a respectful distance apart.

My mother shuffled in and out of the kitchen, bringing out plates of appetizers and pastries she had made. When his parents complimented my mother on what an amazing cook she was, she bragged, "The recipes have been in our family for generations." She told them that she and Tata had also taught them to me. Because it was Christmastime, the house was warm and decorated. Between the food and the festive atmosphere, my mother was showing all of her talents, which reflected positively on me.

I remember my father smiling ear to ear. Every family wanted Malek to marry their daughter, so even though I was young, my father wanted this for me. He knew I would have a good life and would be comfortable financially. And if the most eligible man in our community chose me, at nineteen, it would reflect well on my parents by indicating that they had raised me right, to be the kind of girl who could satisfy the demanding Middle Eastern man's high expectations. As much as I'd been resisting this meeting, I also trusted that my parents loved me and, each for their own reasons, truly wanted the best possible life for their daughter.

Malek stared straight at me. Apart from the two or three months I spent in Nader's company, I was not used to a man looking at me so directly and I felt intimidated. In normal circumstances, this was considered rude; if men around campus or town seemed to be observing me so intently and openly as I walked by, I would have dropped my head in embarrassment and kept moving.

Now, I was expected to communicate with Malek, as handsome as he was, as if this were a casual, comfortable conversation. To make matters worse, we had an audience. He not only observed every move I made, but he also seemed curious and asked me all kinds of questions. He wanted to know about my university, when I expected to graduate. He asked, "Why did you choose to major in economics?"

I answered, "Hummen khassasuni," meaning, the university chose the major for me. Because my grade-point average was not high enough, I could not specialize in business administration, the program that initially interested me. One of the few choices I had, as a result of my performance, included economics. The program was not as demanding as the business program, and I knew I might like economics based on my discussions with Uncle Anton. Compared to agriculture and education, which the university counselor also offered, I was content with this option.

Malek seemed pleased with my response and smiled; to share that the university had chosen my degree for me meant I was not overly ambitious, though I didn't realize the positive sway this held for him at the time. As the conversation continued, I became terrified by the internal shift that had occurred when I first shook Malek's hand and my immediate desire to impress him; I had gone from resisting this meeting to falling for this man in seconds.

To my surprise, while we were talking, Malek pulled out a pack of Marlboro Lights. "Dima, would you like a cigarette?" he asked and extended the open box to me.

Our parents watched in silence, looking back and forth at the interaction between Malek and me.

I was shocked that he would ask me in the presence of my parents if I wanted to smoke, knowing that it was impolite for a daughter to smoke in front of her family. At the same time, it was confirmation that this older, worldly man truly was more Western-minded than the average Middle Eastern man who had never left home.

"No, thank you," I said. "I don't smoke." My answer, which was the truth, broke a silent moment in the room. Both of our parents seemed relieved and smiled with satisfaction, especially my father.

Malek smiled as well. He pulled out a cigarette, put it in his mouth, and lit it while still smiling at me. He told me later that if I had said "yes" in that moment, he would not have wanted to marry me. To accept the cigarette would have indicated that I was more "open" than the kind of girl he was looking for in a wife. I passed his first test.

Amo Dawoud called my father the next day and asked for my hand in marriage for his son. This proposal was my parents' greatest joy. It validated that they had done their job as parents, and done it well. I'd never seen them so proud.

A couple of weeks later, Malek and I shared our first kiss. I remember it distinctly. He came over with his parents for dinner and asked me to accompany him onto our roof. We were walking up the staircase when he leaned into me. I still could not believe that Malek—this man whose charming presence filled an entire room—was attracted to me. I saw myself as a plain, inexperienced girl who had no sense of the world. I wanted to impress him, but as he came closer, I froze.

The second his lips touched mine, I relaxed. The kiss was soft and kind, and I got lost in that kiss. Then, he pulled away from me, looked at my eyes and asked, "Is this your first kiss?"

The nerves shot back through me. I knew that my answer would determine if there was ever going to be a second kiss for us. If he discovered that I had kissed or even had the slightest emotions for another man before him, he would no longer want me; I would no longer be perceived as a newborn kitten with her eyes still closed, naïve with no experiences.

"Yes, it is my first kiss," I said.

"Well, how did you know what to do, then?" he asked.

"I read about it in *Seventeen*, an American magazine," I said, hoping this would be enough. He proceeded to ask, "Can you bring this magazine to me? I would like to see it." I thought he was kidding, but he wasn't.

"I don't remember exactly which issue the kissing article was published in," I said. "I have a lot of them."

"Then, let me see all of your magazines," he said, half teasing and halfway suspicious. He continued up the stairs to the roof, and I went back downstairs to my room. I grabbed my pile of magazines and brought them up to Malek. We spent the next half hour or so rummaging through their pages.

When we found an article with the instructions for French kissing, he finally relaxed, laughed about it, and began flirting with me.

"Well let's test the instructions one more time," he said.

I passed the second test. I was worthy, after all.

One month later, I went with my new fiancé to his shop in the gold market to pick out my jewelry for our engagement party. Before I went, Baba gave me serious advice.

"I know you have simple taste," he said, "but choose heavy pieces, even if they are not your personal style. As you pick the pieces, remember that they represent your worth."

12 *Good Appearances and Bad Omens*

In the beginning of my relationship with Malek, there were many times when I had to keep up appearances in some way or another, times when I had to make sure my glass vase would not appear blemished. These good appearances and bad omens were really just one and the same, though I did not see them this way at the time.

Three months after I accepted Malek's proposal, an anonymous woman called him. She called herself a *Fa'elet Khair*, a "Doer of Good." *Fa'elet Khair*s were common in our community; they were individuals who claimed they were doing something helpful for one person by spreading information that usually harmed another person. She told Malek I had been interested in another man.

Two days before our engagement party, Malek and I had plans to go shopping for his suit and shirt. I was excited to see him and to go shopping with him. Malek called me around 4:30 p.m. He said, "Mean be hibbik?" which means, "Who loves you?" His voice was not friendly, it sounded suspicious and angry, and he was asking other strange questions.

I was in my room standing in front of my closet and trying to decide what I would wear that night. I was talking to him and shuffling through my clothes. I walked to my mother's closet, hoping to find something of hers to wear, when Malek asked again, "Mean be hibbik?"

"What do you mean?" I asked.

"Is it Nader?" he asked.

I froze. I wanted to start our relationship with honesty and trust. Malek had shared many stories of his intimate relationships with past girlfriends. I had enjoyed hearing these stories; they sounded like romantic movies. But my mother had made it clear from the beginning that I should not share anything with Malek about Nader. She warned that Malek would never marry me if I did.

Instead of telling the truth, I answered with more questions. "What do you mean? Who is Nader?" I was relieved he could not see the flushed look on my face at that moment.

"Are you sure you do not know Nader? I heard that he is your love." Malek said, laughing cynically.

I could hardly breathe, but I asked again, "What are you talking about?"

"A woman called me today. She refused to give me her name. She said she was a *Fa'elet Khair*," Malek said. "She told me that you are in love with Nader, and he is your classmate. She said that your mother forced you to end the relationship."

I was not sure if I should open up and tell Malek the truth, or if I should continue denying everything. I acted like I knew nothing.

As soon as I hung up, my mother arrived home from work. She was walking to her room to change out of her work clothes. I grabbed her arm and took her aside to my room. We closed the door and sat on my bed. I was panicking and slapping my right cheek over and over. She looked shocked and asked, "Sho fee?" What is happening?

"Malek knows about Nader," I said. "I want to tell him the

truth. I did not do anything wrong, and I want our relationship to start with honesty and trust," I said, still upset.

My mother grabbed hold of my hands and looked at me with a serious expression. Firmly and calmly, she said, "Listen to me, Dima. Don't you dare tell him a thing. If he finds out that you had *any* interest in another man, even if you did not do anything wrong, he will not want you anymore. Then what will you tell your father? How would you explain this to our community? If Malek leaves you because of this, no other man will want you, either." She looked at me, still holding my hands steady, and she said, "Act like you know nothing. Act like the other woman is not telling the truth."

So I did. To tell him the truth would have cost us our wedding and humiliated my family.

Malek had planned a big engagement party. Aromatic candles and flower bouquets decorated the centers of the tables. The tables surrounded the edges of a ballroom dance floor. The chairs had been covered in crisp, white fabric. We had a formal, seated dinner. A band played Arabic music for us and for hundreds of our family members and friends. It was like a fairy tale or a scene out of a romance movie. I was thankful and overjoyed to have hope for a better life and better marriage than the one I witnessed between my parents.

Malek and I were excited to be officially together and to celebrate our new relationship with our relatives. At the party, the pastor made our engagement official by praying for our unity. Then, in front of everyone, Malek gifted me the gold jewelry that we had chosen together in his shop—a necklace, earrings, rings, a bracelet, and the engagement band. He helped me put it all on, and I heard a nearby older woman whisper in a pleased voice, "He is covering her up in gold."

In the excitement that evening, we kissed multiple times. The kisses were captured on video and camera, and I imagined they would remind us of this beautiful night. I considered the kisses to be a gesture of love; I considered it normal for an engaged couple to express feelings for one another.

My father was not pleased. He was initially thrilled when Malek's father asked him for my hand in marriage for his son. That night, as he watched Malek and me kissing, he did not want the engagement anymore.

He managed to stay calm in front of the guests, but when the party ended just after midnight, as my mother, brother, sister, and I got in the car to drive home, he immediately started yelling. "I'm going to hide a meat knife in the plant next to our front door," he screamed. "When Malek comes to pick you up tomorrow, I am going to stab him in his chest!" He screamed the entire drive home. He had had several whiskeys on the rocks at the party. We were terrified, not just because of his screaming but because he was driving out of control, barely avoiding multiple accidents.

That night, I hadn't fulfilled his expectations of an innocent girl or a pure daughter. I hadn't acted in public the way he thought I should have. He accused me of bringing him shame in front of our community because I had kissed Malek. As irrational as his reaction was, beneath it, I could detect the fear of losing his first and oldest daughter. He was trying to hold on to his role as a father and keep me in my role as his little girl, but he didn't know how. Sadly, for both of us, the only way he could manifest his fear and pain was through toxic, controlling behavior.

As he sped through the streets to our home, he shouted, "I'm going to take away every piece of gold Malek's family has given to you." This was the same jewelry he'd advised me to pick out carefully, for its elaborate embellishment and weight, for its determination of my worth. He continued, "I'll take it to his parents' home and throw it in their faces."

I was angry and devastated, but screaming back at him was not an option. I cried in silence, the way I'd been conditioned to cry. I listened to the words flying out of his mouth and felt terrified that my engagement might end.

The next morning, he woke up seemingly calm and composed. He walked up to the roof, as he usually did, to drink the coffee my mother had already prepared for him and to smoke from his hookah. We couldn't tell if he was still angry from the night before, if we should try to mend what had happened, or if we should just act normal. So, we acted normal.

The night of my engagement party was the first of many screaming bouts, rages, and fights that occurred every weekend. This routine continued for over a year until my wedding day finally arrived. I had foolishly fantasized that the engagement period was the happiest time for couples. For Malek and me, it was filled with family conflict and terror.

My father changed my curfew from four in the afternoon to ten at night, but this curfew became a game of tug-of-war. Malek used to pick me up around 6:30 or 7:00 p.m., after he had finished work. If I arrived home past 10:00 p.m.—ten minutes late, five minutes late, two minutes late—the number of minutes did not matter, I was in deep trouble.

The first time I was late, my father decided to teach all of us a lesson. He threatened to end the engagement, and my mom and my uncles had to convince him not to.

At the same time, Malek knew my curfew, but he used to prolong our dates, taking his time to finish his drink or to pay the bill, taking the long way on an evening stroll, anything to push my arrival time just a few minutes past ten o'clock to send a message to my father.

The two of them were like fencers engaged in a match of intimidation and control, each using his sword to show dominance. Their goal, I think, was less about controlling me and more about demonstrating who was the more powerful man; I was just an object in this competition. Early on, the game of power was masked in seemingly simple matters, like a curfew. But in my experience, even simple matters are not simple.

As soon as I left for the evening, to avoid the out-of-control reaction from my father, my mother started sneaking around the house winding the clocks back—in the kitchen, in the bedroom, anywhere there was a clock. She even wound my father's watch back after he placed it on the bedside table. The second I walked through the door, she would whisper angrily, "Where have you been? Are you trying to cause another fight?" Then, once my father was sound asleep, she would go around again, winding the clocks forward, making the time right.

Each and every time my father threatened to end the engagement, he was dead serious, until either we promised not to disobey him or until his mood and composure seemed suddenly restored. He kept me in a constant cycle of fear followed by false relief. He had the power to end what I believed was the one hope I had for a better future.

Whatever resistance I originally had to the idea of getting married young had completely dissolved. Just as my mother carefully watched our clocks to keep me out of trouble, I carefully watched the calendar, counting down the months and days. Not only was I in love with Malek, but my father's erratic actions were also driving my desire to get out of this house that was filled with his fury. I was waiting nervously and patiently for my wedding day.

Perhaps the greatest and most obvious omen of all was this one, which went back much further than my engagement: I knew, despite appearances, that all of the women in my family were deeply miserable. The particular brand of misery had been handed down to each generation, over and over, with stories like the one about the perfect glass vase and all of the threatening expectations that came with the story, trapping them in their misery.

The entirety of my engagement, instead of feeling happy, I stepped lightly, trying to avoid hidden grenades at every turn. As a result, before my wedding day arrived and without conscious recognition, I took my place in this generational misery.

13 ⟩ *A Spring Day*

April 28, 1996: Outside, a sunny morning, a clear blue sky. The doorbell ringing over and over with fragrant flower bouquet deliveries. Inside, pink, peach, and white blooming in every space.

I am twenty, with only two and a half years of university complete, and I am anticipating beginning the rest of my life. I wake up early humming Arabic tunes, songs played over and over at the celebratory gatherings we've been hearing over the last two weeks. Each night, at a different family member's home, the same love songs played.

The house is full: Baba; Mama; my sister, Ruba; Auntie Nadia; and her husband, Sami, who flew in from Canada; and Uncle Anton, who came from the United States. Only my brother, Waseem, who has recently moved to the United States, is unable to fly back for the wedding.

When I first called Uncle Anton to share that I had agreed to marry Malek, he sounded disappointed. He had hoped that I would graduate first. Regardless, he is here, supporting me and participating in the celebration.

In the early afternoon, the hairdresser and the makeup artist finish helping me get ready, and I put on my wedding dress that we ordered from the States. I have been trying it on for months. This is the first time I have worn a dress that leaves my shoulders bare. This, alone, feels liberating. I am covered in hundreds of tiny pearls—the beading on the dress, the necklace, the earrings, and the bracelet.

As I walk out, family members greet me and hug me, one by one. Mama and Auntie Nadia are crying in a corner and trying not to mess up their makeup. The photographer is trying to capture every hug while the hairdresser follows me around with a bottle of hairspray. I sit in the center of the guest room. One by one, parents, aunts, uncles, and kids walk to me and take a picture as they gift me with gold jewelry.

When the doorbell rings at four o'clock, my father rushes to the door. "Malek's parents are here," he says.

My heart beats with anticipation. This is the tradition: The groom's parents and closest family members come to the bride's home to accompany her to the church. Malek's father and mother walk through the door, followed by about twenty of Malek's aunts, cousins, and relatives. Between my family and Malek's family, there are forty or fifty people in our home. They all blend together, shaking hands and hugging, saying, "Mabrook!" Congratulations!

There are not enough chairs to accommodate everyone. Out of respect, my family gives priority to Malek's family to sit. Mama and Auntie Nadia walk around with silver trays filled with glasses of champagne and chocolates. When everyone has champagne and a chocolate, we toast. Baba and Amo Dawoud stand and shake each other's hands, signifying that I can now leave my parents' home.

I can finally leave my father's restrictions and the years of pain hidden beneath an unblemished exterior. I can forget the weekly fights and my father's threats to break Malek and me apart. I can forget their power struggles; I can forget the fear and tension. I am about to be liberated from the past. Malek represents freedom, a modern lifestyle, an abundance of opportunities, and also joy. He is like a savior transitioning me out of a painful past and giving me a chance to enter a new life far away. The moment that Baba and Amo Dawoud shake hands, with smiles wide across their faces, I belong to Malek's family.

Sound of joy! Sound of celebration! *"Lu lu lu lu lu lu lu, lu lu lu lu, lu lu lu lu lu lu lu luleeeesh—"* five older women, two from my side of the family and three from Malek's side, stand up and start singing the *zagareet*, a repeated, quivering trill; a quick roll of the tongue; a steady cluck; fast, fast, fast, a silk ribbon unraveling; a holler into a tunnel; an echo from a mountaintop. *"Lu lu lu lu lu lu, lu lu lu lu, lu lu lu lu lu lu lu luleeeesh—"* the sound of the women's voices fills the entire house and stairwell as I walk down, leaving my parents' home, step by step, next to Amo Dawoud, until I am outside at the street to greet the procession. A warm, sunny day. A clear blue sky.

Cars line the narrow street in front of my parents' home and block traffic. The white Mercedes limousine that Malek rented for the day is at the front of the line and is decorated with flowers. I step out onto the street, and cars begin honking in unison until I get into the limo with my two bridesmaids and my sister. This is one of the traditions I love most. I have heard these beeps for other brides since I was a little girl, when I would run to the closest window and fling open the curtains to look at the colorful procession of cars following the white car at the front, decorated with flowers. I would strain to catch a glimpse of the bride inside the car. Today, the beeping is for me, for my decorated white car; some other young children are in their windows trying to get a glimpse of me in my wedding dress, as I'm sitting in the backseat and smiling out the window.

We drive down the narrow, curving old roads of Amman, past ancient, white, square buildings that look like rising dust particles of a long history shining in a sunray, vibrant against a blue sky. We arrive at the Anglican Church where I will be married. The limo driver parks. About thirty feet away, I see Malek standing confidently between his two cousins, the bishop, and the pastor in a big courtyard in front of the church gate. When I get out of the car, I walk through an archway decorated with flowers and into the courtyard.

I have been patiently anticipating this day. I am ready to begin my liberated life in the United States with Malek.

In one photograph that has always stayed with me, my father is walking me down the aisle. In my memory, he is frowning. But in reality, the picture captures a slight smile that looks to me like a mix of pride for the occasion and the prestigious match and sadness for losing his oldest daughter. With every step we take, I see faces I have known since I was a little girl; they are all looking at my dad and me. The pastor's son plays the piano as we get closer to the altar.

Gray-haired men with thick mustaches and dark suits. Dark-haired women wearing their most prized gold jewelry and silk suits that they will trade out for colorful dresses after the ceremony. Wooden pews decorated with more peach, pink, and white flowers and tied with white ribbons. The church walls are empty, clean, and white, with no statues of Jesus or the Virgin Mary, and none of the colorful stained glass that I am accustomed to seeing in my Catholic church.

I am holding my bouquet in my left hand and, with my right hand, holding my father's arm. I have a big smile, made even more visible with my red lipstick. In the photo, my smile is the biggest in the room. My eyes are looking ahead, directly at Malek. I remember my joy and smile growing with every step that brings me closer to him. In that moment, seemingly suspended in time by the photograph, I am thanking God and the Virgin Mary that this wedding is finally happening.

14　An American Dream

My mother and Tata believe in the power of dreams. They discuss their dreams and interpret the possible meanings frequently. I learned at an early age about simple symbols: a fish means good luck; a mouse means someone will try to steal from me; a cat means someone will betray me; raw meat means someone close will die; a woman wearing a wedding dress is bad luck; a pregnant woman means that a person is carrying a lot of worry.

I have many of my own dreams. There is one I have when I am about twelve, and though I cannot interpret it at the time, it remains vivid in my memory for many years. It turns out to be a transformative vision of my life to come.

In the dream, I am standing in the kitchen at our home and looking out the window at Jabal al Hussain in the distance, one of the seven hills that Amman was originally founded on in 7250 BC. I see my small world from the third floor. All the homes are made of white limestone, tinted gray from history and city smog; each home has a television antenna and a water tank on its flat roof. The two-, three-, and four-story houses appear to be stacked next to each other like carved rectangles rising out of white stone. Observed from above, the ancient, narrow streets that separate city blocks look like winding crevices etched into this landscape of white limestone.

In my heart, I long for vibrant trees and grassy hills and wildflowers, to be surrounded by a lush landscape. I crave something I have only ever seen in pictures in magazines.

I am wearing blue jeans and a red T-shirt. I turn away from the window and walk to the wooden kitchen cabinets. I stand next to the cabinets and the fridge that always seems to be leaking. I open one of the lower cabinets. Inside, I find a tunnel. It is short, only about two arms' length. I can easily see a bright light at its end. I squeeze in without closing the cabinet door behind me, and I crawl to the other side.

I can see a warm, assuring bright light. When I reach the end and step out, there is no one there. I am standing on the other side, and I have a clear, certain sense of where I am. I've left my kitchen in Amman, and I have arrived in a land of trees, hills, grass, and dreams. I am in America, and I know that I want to stay here.

15 Little Middle East

If you peek inside most homes in Jordan, you'll see expensive tile floors covered with Persian rugs woven with intricate flower patterns; heavy wooden furniture with ornate engravings; brown, burgundy, and navy couches with decorative throw pillows with the traditional Jordanian and Palestinian red cross-stitched covers; a turned-on television in the background; ashtrays set out for smokers; crystal vases and dishes; and framed photographs displayed on tabletops that are covered with crocheted trivets. There's a feeling of formality blended with comfort. There is heaviness in the air; maybe it is the weight of expectations and appearances that must be kept, or maybe it is the weight of hidden secrets.

Now blink quickly. When you open your eyes, you're halfway around the globe in my small Arab community in San Diego. But you wouldn't believe you're not still in Amman. Just as beliefs and traditional thinking are strictly preserved when my community members immigrate to the United States, so are their taste in furniture and the feel of their homes.

Families that can't afford Persian rugs fill their homes with knockoffs that look similar, but these rugs never have the same soft, silky feel under bare feet. The Arabic channel is always on television; Al Jazeera is covering the latest Middle East news, showing old movies, the latest Arabic sitcoms, dramatic series, and music videos.

When family members and friends visit each others' homes, they sit drinking Lipton tea boiled with mint freshly picked from the garden. It is served in traditional tea glasses, small, clear glasses decorated with gold rims and geometric or scrolled patterns with matching saucers underneath. On the side of the plate, especially around holidays, there is a homemade *ma'moul* cookie. A plate filled with chocolates is placed in the middle of the coffee table on top of a crocheted place mat that an aunt or grandmother made by hand.

The only immediate difference between these homes, separated by oceans, is the big windows. In San Diego, in the one- or two-story suburban homes, the windows that bring in an abundance of sunlight are free from decorative iron bars intended to stop thieves from entering the homes in Amman.

When we arrived in the States, I wanted to rent an apartment in a newly built complex that was fifteen minutes away from the home Malek's parents had purchased, but he immediately struck the possibility. "Oh, that would be too far to drive," he said, as if the idea of living just a few miles apart was a drastic distance. Instead, Malek rented a one-bedroom apartment in Rancho Bernardo, a community in the northern hills of San Diego, just twenty miles from the beach.

Amo Dawoud and Amto Kasma were disappointed that Malek and I rented our own apartment. They had purchased a three-bedroom house, where Malek's brother and sister-in-law were living. His parents planned to move to the United States in a year and imagined that both of their sons and daughters-in-law and future grandchildren would live with them in the house.

The apartment we rented was not even a four-minute drive to his parents' house; only a golf course separated our homes. We also lived less than two minutes away from Malek's sister's house, and her own in-laws lived all around her. Here we all were, on a completely different continent but living very short distances from one another; this was common practice in our Little Middle East. The entire community existed within a fifteen-mile radius. It took one person to emigrate from Jordan to Rancho Bernardo sixty years earlier, and all the other community members that immigrated afterward moved into the same area.

The only family members from my side of the marriage who lived in San Diego were Auntie Mariam and her four grown children. Auntie Mariam was my father's distant cousin, and she reached out to me when I arrived in San Diego. But from the beginning, Malek did not want me to interact with her or with her family. He did not want me to have any family influence that was not from his family. So while I visited openly with Malek's sister and sister-in-law, if I stopped by Auntie Mariam's apartment, I kept it from Malek.

Just as Tata had visited her friends weekly, community members visited each other weekly in Rancho Bernardo. In *this* Little Middle East, the men discussed the effects of American foreign policy on the Middle East and shared news not covered on CNN that they heard from family members in Jordan. The women gossiped about boys and girls acting too American and not following their fathers' orders. I remember hearing about a woman named Leila who made her son get married at the age of eighteen to the eighteen-year-old daughter of a family friend. The two did not know each other well and were an unfit couple, but Leila was terrified that her son would have multiple girlfriends once he started college, and as a result, he would get AIDS. So she married him off right after high school. In addition to these kinds of scandals, the women talked about the latest news about who had gotten engaged, married, or pregnant or who had died. This closeness to one another and to the culture created a sense of safety and a support structure that prevented Middle Eastern children from totally disappearing into the big American melting pot.

At first, I lived in the moment, enjoying each experience. Everything was new—I was a new wife, in a new community, in a new country. It felt like Malek and I had been given a blank canvas onto which we could paint whatever life we wanted.

I was a married woman in the United States learning from a man who knew so much about the world, and a man whom I loved. We honeymooned in Hawaii. We went out for sushi and to the movies. He took me gambling in casinos. He explained his views on politics and religion. He taught me about intimacy by sharing stories and experiences from relationships he had had with ex-girlfriends. He helped me overcome my fear of driving on the freeway and my frustration in understanding Americans as they spoke so fast. We loved to bake together. We would make *manakish bi' za'atar* pastry. Malek would roll the dough thin, getting it just right for me to add the *za'atar*—a filling of Middle Eastern herbs, sesame seeds, and olive oil mixed together. I was having more fun than I'd ever had in my life. Malek was opening my eyes to the world, and anything he did or said seemed perfect in my mind. I was hungry and grateful for his lessons. I looked up to and adored Malek; I thought of him as my teacher and friend.

I was seeing what I wanted and hoped to see: that Malek and I were designing something together on our fresh, blank canvas. I couldn't yet see that the structure and traditions of this community, that replicated life in Amman, already predetermined our lifestyle and relationship dynamic. Still rooted in my social constructs and my earliest romantic ideas, in spite of everything that came before and after we married, I loved Malek.

16 ⟩ *Love and Destruction*

As a young girl and teenager, I tried to make sense of my father's rages, but I couldn't. I once asked Uncle Jaffar, my father's brother, "Why is Baba so tough? Why does he scream all the time?"

"Because he loves you," my uncle said.

"What do you mean?" I asked.

"The female cat, when she gives birth to the kittens—" my uncle answered, "she loves them so much that she eats them." The words were not reassuring at all, but they came out of his mouth so comfortably and casually.

I grew up hearing many misleading statements, lies that posed as facts. Anger and violence were always linked to love. It didn't matter what the relationship was—father and daughter, husband and wife, father-in-law and son-in-law, mother-in-law and daughter-in-law. I grew up with the unconscious, ingrained belief that there was a natural connection between love and manipulation, love and abuse, love and complete destruction.

Even so, I thought my relationship with Amto Kasma would be better than the one that my mother had with her mother-in-law. After all, Malek's mother had handpicked me for her son; she thought we would be a good match. Soon I understood what "a good match" meant to her, and I learned that it hurt her to see other couples happy—even her own sons and daughters-in-law.

Just before our wedding, I had a phone conversation with Amto Kasma. "Malek and I are planning to drive to the Dead Sea to stay at one of the new resorts for a few days after the wedding," I told her, excited to share our plans. I imagined that we would float together in the salt-saturated water and cover ourselves with the mineral-rich dark mud; we would relax as a couple for the very first time without worrying about being ten minutes late to a curfew. Finally, we could make decisions and plans together without any external controls.

But Amto Kasma said, "No. You're not going to the Dead Sea. *Aib*, you should stay in Amman and spend time with our family before you fly to San Diego." Then calmly and seriously, she explained, "Just like your father controlled you while you were engaged, I am going to control you once you get married."

I was shocked. I didn't know how to respond, so I swallowed and said nothing.

That afternoon, Malek called me. "My mother stopped by my office," he said, "and she explained something that I was unaware of."

"What?" I asked, unsure what she could have said.

"If a new bride goes to the Dead Sea right after her wedding night, she'll get an infection; it is like pouring salt on a wound in a delicate area." He continued, "My mother loves you and cares for you as if you are her daughter, so she has recommended that we stay in Amman instead."

This was yet another false test of my character and worth based on a misleading lie delivered as if it were a scientific fact. It was an old wives' tale that if a bride went to the Dead Sea and did not get an infection, it would prove that she was not a virgin. If I insisted on going, my mother-in-law could accuse me of being impure, even though there was no truth to this belief. Malek canceled the trip to the Dead Sea.

Another time, I asked Amto Kasma to share her recipe for one of Malek's favorite meals. It was a traditional dish made from lamb spleens stuffed with parsley and garlic. I attempted the recipe she gave me, following each step, only to find that she'd purposely left out one very important detail: to make deep gashes in the spleens with a knife before parboiling them so they wouldn't explode. I learned later that she omitted this detail on purpose. When her other daughter-in-law had pointed out to Amto Kasma that she'd left out this step, she told her, "It will be a good lesson for Dima to learn on her own."

My mother-in-law had a difficult marriage with almost no privacy. When she first moved into her husband's home, she moved into a house with her mother-in-law and five sisters-in-law. They all lived in a three-bedroom and one-bathroom home. Then she gave birth to three children, two sons and a daughter. Over the years, four of the sisters-in-law got married and moved out, but by then, Amto Kasma's youth had passed.

Malek's father was the only son and the youngest sibling. He felt responsible for his mother and sisters from an early age, since his father had passed away when he was young. He succeeded in supporting them by starting his business selling small pieces of gold jewelry on a rug on the street in front of the gold market. Eventually, he built it up, became known for his competitive prices, and purchased his own shop.

I asked my mother-in-law many times why my father-in-law didn't rent a separate home for his mother once he could afford to. "Aib," my mother-in-law always answered. To rent a separate home would have been shameful; it would look as if my father-in-law didn't want to care for his mother and was discarding her. To satisfy what the community would think about him, Malek's

parents lived in discomfort for most of their married lives. My
mother-in-law expected me to live in the same discomfort, and
when I disagreed, she considered it disrespectful.

More often than not, Amto Kasma exercised her control over
me through small manipulations, bending and twisting the truth
in ways that pitted my husband and me against each other. This
became a recurring pattern. To the best of her ability, my mother-
in-law maintained her promise to control me inside my marriage.

The success or failure of my marriage to Malek did not rest
solely on Amto Kasma, any more than it rested solely on my father. Malek and I bore the real responsibility.

As the smallest pebble quietly splashes the surface of the water
in a deep well, I have a glimmer of an awakening, a realization:
my marriage had been a transaction between owners; I had been
transferred from one man to another, from my father to my husband. An experience early in my marriage shows me this truth,
but it takes a long time before I can put the realization into words.

It is May 1996. I am twenty years old, and I have been married for one month. I am sitting next to Malek at the kitchen table, looking at him with admiration and pride.

I ask, "What do you love most about me?" I'm hoping to be
flattered, hoping he'll express his love for me with the kinds of
phrases I heard in songs that played on the radio in my grandmother's kitchen when I was a child. "Why did you choose me to
be your wife?" I ask.

Without having to think about his answer, he confidently re-
plies, "I like how naïve and inexperienced you are. That's why
my parents introduced me to you." He takes a drag of his ciga-

rette and looks me in the eyes before saying, "My dad thought you were perfect for me, because you are like a blob of dough that I can shape. I didn't want to marry someone in her mid-twenties who already had a developed personality, who was already educated and knew what she wanted in life. I was looking for a young woman whom I could shape."

I look closely at Malek's big brown eyes, hoping to find that he is joking. It has to be a joke—a silly joke about the unconscious fears that he is seeing in me. I have never once thought that being naïve and easily shaped could be perceived as my most attractive qualities. However, his eyes look firm and direct; they confirm quickly that there is no humor in his response.

This isn't the romantic confession of love I'd hoped to hear. I watch smoke swirl around his hands and face. I am disappointed, devastated even, not to hear the language of shining stars and blooming flowers pour off Malek's tongue.

Yet at that moment I know that I am the right fit for the role. My upbringing prepared me to be the dough. I am not offended or insulted. Any man in my community would have expected the same as Malek, and in truth, he never made promises of anything different. While my identity is molded before I ever have the chance to discover its true form, I am happy to be a part of Malek's life.

For a long time, I believed familial love and brutal destruction came together in a single package. This was the way I'd been raised. When I was sixteen, I read *Romeo and Juliet* in school and then watched the movie. I was captivated, because I wasn't accustomed to seeing passionate romances play out before my eyes. I didn't exist in a culture in which dating was the norm or where it was acceptable for romances to blossom without parental consent.

After I watched this movie, I hoped for that kind of passionate love. With no relationship experience and no strong models of relationships free from complications, seeing Romeo and Juliet fall in love and then die for one another against the backdrop of their feuding families made sense; it fit with the idea that with love came destruction. It was easy to incorporate the notions of love at first sight, forbidden love, and passion with the basic belief that love and destruction went hand in hand, just as Uncle Jaffar had once explained.

From the moment I shook Malek's hand on the day we met, I thought I had experienced love at first sight. It's true that our families put us together. It's true that I felt I would be marrying into financial security. It's true that even though I'd hoped to graduate first, I thought marriage was the next normal step in my life at that point. By all practical measures, we fit together, but I also believed, after meeting him, that he was my very own Romeo.

Once we were engaged, the fact that my father and Malek's family were constantly at odds felt dramatic, but also natural. Love came with destruction. Families feuded. Real lovers were sometimes "star-crossed."

When we made it to the altar, I thought we had made it to our own storybook ending—to a different outcome than the one Romeo and Juliet had and, in fact, to a beautiful, hopeful beginning.

17 *Account Balances*

Balance was the core issue in my marriage: the balance of trust, the balance of anger and jealousy, and the balance of power. From the beginning, not just the beginning of our marriage, but from the beginning of our engagement, there was no balance—there was only imbalance. As I began to evolve, the imbalance became more pronounced and less bearable. I take responsibility for that fact, but I don't regret my growth.

Before I got married, I did not think of marriage as a partnership. My idea of marriage was a fantasy: it was having a nice wedding, having a nice house, and keeping it clean. I thought it was a man's responsibility to take care of me financially. My idea of marriage was not complicated, but it was naïve. It was based on movies, and nothing else.

Then I experienced a major shift. I realized I wanted a partner, and I wanted to *be* a partner. This shift didn't occur in one moment or one day; it occurred over years.

After we got engaged, we had many important conversations. There is one that stands out in my memory.

It is common for Middle Eastern families to hope for the virgin bride to become pregnant on her wedding night. But Uncle Anton's words about marriage, children, and education echoed between my ears. One evening, before my parents called Uncle Anton to tell him about my engagement, Malek and I were sitting on the rooftop.

I said, "I have to talk to you about something serious."

"What is it?" he asked, and he removed a box of cigarettes from his shirt pocket.

"I am nervous that I will disappoint Uncle Anton. He has always had such a big hope for me to be the first educated woman in our family." At the time, I felt safe saying these things to Malek.

He took a drag from his cigarette and then casually exhaled smoke as he responded. "If you want to be the first educated woman in your family, you will be," he said.

I wasn't convinced he understood how serious I was, so I said to him, "I want your word that you will let me finish my degree before we have children."

Malek looked into my eyes and said, "Dima, you have my word."

I felt relieved. I exhaled and felt myself relax. "Okay," I said. "Thank you."

He nodded slightly as he took another long drag from his cigarette. After he finished, he put it out in the ashtray on the table in front of us. He leaned toward me and said, "Now, I have to talk to you about something."

"What is it?" I asked, suddenly feeling nervous again.

He spoke slowly and deliberately. "I have to warn you: I am a jealous man, I cannot trust people, and I have a temper. Can you handle that?"

I felt so honored that this man seemed to be sharing his deepest secrets with me. Eager to please and satisfy my fiancé, and certain that I could, I smiled at what I mistook as a confession. "*Habibi*, my love, you will never have any reason not to trust me," I reassured him.

I imagined that once he was with me long enough, he would

come to trust me, and his temper would dissipate. Of course, that didn't happen. His lack of trust, his jealousy, and his temper surfaced early in our relationship, but I didn't fully recognize them for what they were. At first, I interpreted these characteristics as protective instead of controlling.

To his credit, Malek kept his word and supported my educational aspirations, but he was firm and direct about each of our responsibilities in the marriage. He would earn the household income and pay all of the bills, including my tuition. In return, he expected me to take care of our home and him and to get myself ready to become pregnant as soon as I graduated. It made sense to me. These were the gender roles we were both accustomed to.

Instead of involving me in our financial knowledge or decisions, as soon as we were in the United States, Malek gave me my own financial responsibility to focus on. He took me to open my first bank account and set me up with a monthly allowance. It seemed generous at first.

The day Malek took me to Bank of America left a clear mark in my memory. He had high-dollar accounts, which gave him VIP status. So when we went in, someone ushered us into a private office. Malek had his own personal banker. To my surprise, his personal banker was a woman. She wore a power suit and looked Malek directly in the eyes as she spoke with him. I was completely unaccustomed to seeing a woman in what I perceived to be a powerful position—discussing and handling a man's finances.

After we did the paperwork, Malek handed the account manager three hundred dollars in cash. This would be my monthly allowance to cover my personal expenses. The account manager called a teller to the office. The teller looked like she was about the same age as I was, almost twenty-one. I was fascinated when I observed the female account manager hand this younger woman the three hundred dollars; she was being trusted with the money and was responsible for opening my account. That day, Malek showed me how to write a check and balance a checkbook. After observing the two women in the bank, this small lesson in self-sufficiency felt like a gift.

We went to purchase cars the same week. Not only was Malek well-off on his own, but his father had given us ten thousand dollars as a wedding gift. First, we looked at cars for him, and he bought himself a brand-new red Audi; he spent thirty-three thousand dollars in cash on this indulgence. Then we went shopping for my car. One of the cars we saw was a used Oldsmobile with high mileage. It was big and beige, and I hated it immediately. I was twenty, and I thought it looked like an old person's car. It was so old and such a basic model that it had nothing electric, not even a built-in radio, while Malek's Audi had all the bells and whistles.

I convinced Malek to look at a Honda I liked. It was a brand-new car and cost about twelve thousand dollars. My sister-in-law liked the same car. Malek's brother suggested that they buy two of the Hondas at once, one for each of us, with the idea that they would each get a good deal. Malek refused. Instead, he bought the five thousand–dollar Oldsmobile, which often broke down, many times on the freeway during rush hour, and played no music. Malek told me, "Don't worry, I have an old tape recorder that you can put in the car."

I loved that Malek was handsome and financially secure, and I loved that he was "teaching" me how to live in my new country. But he had made it clear that the money was his and that he was the decision maker in our relationship. So even though I wanted a nicer car, I told myself I should feel grateful for his lessons and generosity. This situation marked the beginning of events that continued to highlight the imbalance of roles and worth throughout our marriage.

Our second year together, I resumed my undergraduate studies at San Diego State University. The same year, Malek's parents moved from Jordan to San Diego. Anytime I got sick or tired, my mother-in-law would exclaim, "You're pregnant! You're pregnant!" Every time she came to our house, or anytime we visited at her home, before we parted ways, she would look at me and say, "May God gift you with a son." Malek and I both felt the pressure.

By this time, my personal allowance of three hundred dollars covered the cost of two items: purchasing gas for my car so I could commute to and from school and purchasing international calling cards so I could speak to my family in Jordan. All of these facts were wrapped up in contention that grew.

We started arguing, and with each month that passed, the arguments became more frequent. Our worst arguments were usually the first week of every month, when we got the phone bill in the mail. I felt isolated in a foreign country and needed to connect with my parents, and the only option other than phone calls was writing letters, which took a month to be delivered in the mail. By then, all the news was old news.

At the time, international calls were charged by the minute and quickly added up. Malek placed a strict monthly budget on our phone bill. He permitted me to talk to my parents for about twenty minutes every Saturday morning to minimize the expense. The monthly budget also included his calls to his family in Jordan, but in his situation, there were no weekly time limits.

To me, it seemed that just by dialing in and saying, "Hello," the twenty minutes were somehow over. Even relying on the calling cards I purchased out of my allowance, I exceeded Malek's household allotment for the phone bill every week and felt anxious all month long, every month, as I waited for the bill to arrive and the fight that would ensue.

During these arguments, he sometimes shouted, "I am not a bank that can afford all of your international phone expenses."

Through school, I had access to e-mail for the first time. At some point, I told Malek, "Fine. You won't have to worry about it anymore. I opened an e-mail account. I'll be able to communicate with my parents more often at no cost to you."

However, this made him angrier, and I couldn't understand why. I thought we'd been arguing about the expense, and I'd found a way around it with e-mail.

Finally, he expressed his anger very clearly. "All along," he screamed, "I wanted to limit your communication with your parents. I do not want them to influence you or our marriage!"

The reality that his restriction had nothing to do with our finances, and only to do with his desire for control, hit me like a slap in the face. While I was barely allowed to speak to my parents, he felt so responsible for ensuring that his parents were okay that he'd made us live within a mile of them. He used to stop by his parents' home daily on his way to work and then again, on his way back from work. His mother drove with him to his office multiple days a week and spent the day there trying to stay involved and informed of everything that was going on.

When the fight ended, he sat in his chair in front of the television. He turned up the volume so it would drown out any other sound. Staring silently at the screen, he lit one cigarette after another, until the living room was a gray cloud of smoke.

I started to question my role in our relationship. As I became more established in my new country, I faced not only culture shock but also a shock over my self-worth. Here I was married to a jeweler who had showered me with gold when we got engaged, but when I looked around, I saw that American women were not wearing the gold jewelry that I was used to seeing. I realized that here, gold did not signify my worth. I ended up putting my jewelry in a safe deposit box and wearing it only when we were invited to weddings or big events.

Instead, an unreliable, unattractive, worn-out car reminded me of my worth. I was not just lost in translation between the English and Arabic languages; I was also lost in expressing my worth in this new culture. I began to ask myself a question: if it isn't gold and it isn't a car, what is the source and representation of my *true* worth? This question led me to ask other questions about my identity and the external and internal expectations and judgments that consumed my life.

I began to feel unsafe and insecure, even though I was supposed to feel secure under Malek's "protection." I had no clue about our finances beyond my allowance. When I asked to know about our financial situation, he would say, "I do not believe that the wife should access information about finances or be informed about the husband's business matters." But he shared all this financial information with his brother and parents. He used his parents' address as his mailing address to keep all his information away from my reach; no piece of mail with his name on it, other than our apartment utility bills, was delivered to our home. I realized that if Malek suddenly got in an accident and died, I would have no financial protection. If something happened, he would not be there to make a three hundred–dollar deposit the following month. I would be at the mercy of my in-laws.

A lot of women would have loved this life. I had seen many women get married, have children, stay home, cook, and clean. I didn't want to live in that mold.

One day, while I was walking on campus, I recognized a familiar face. I had been in the States for nearly two years, and I had been at San Diego State University for a full year. I saw the teller who had been called to the account manager's office in Bank of America the very first time I went there with Malek. She was the young woman who had been handed the deposit. Here was the teller, around the same age as I was, who had been in her business attire that day and who had handled my money.

Now she was dressed like the other American students. She wore jeans and a T-shirt and carried a backpack full of books slung over her arm. I saw her face and remembered her right away. At that moment, it occurred to me that she was not just a teller whom I had looked up to as if she were a strange object; she was an empowered American woman working to advance herself. I felt thrilled and smiled in her direction. I was not just smiling at her; I was smiling at all the possibility that she suddenly represented. I told myself, *I wish I could be like her, independent and confident.*

18) *A Shattered Vase*

On my graduation day from San Diego State in May 1999 and three years into my marriage, I woke up proud of my accomplishment. I spent the morning getting ready the way my parents had spent the day getting ready for Malek's first visit to our home. I had purchased a new dress and new sandals. I spent time fixing my hair and makeup and choosing the right jewelry to wear with my new clothes. The graduation game that Tata invented in her kitchen was about to become my reality. I was excited to wear my black cap and gown, and I could not wait to receive my real diploma.

Malek did not share my joy. He was more calm and quiet than usual that day, but he also looked for reasons to start arguments. Sitting in the car, just before we drove to the ceremony, he decided to put me in my place. He said, "I hope you don't think that you will start acting independent with this degree of yours."

I was stunned. It was as if he'd put a dark stain on a clean, white cloth. Even though Malek had been open to my completing my degree, he did not understand how significant the accomplishment was for me. Instead, he was worried about how my accomplishment might affect him. He had his own insecurities; he worried that I might rise above his control. He had also been shaped by our culture to fit a mold with certain expectations that defined his manhood and identity, and he was afraid his role as a man would be undermined.

With a degree, I could get a good-paying job and stop depending solely on the monthly allowance. I'd be able to afford expenses that he'd had full control over, such as the phone bill. I could also start contributing income to our household expenses. But my greatest joy came from feeling good about my accomplishment, building my confidence, and meeting new people who would continue to influence my growth. All of this was threatening to Malek; he could sense the possibility of the balance tipping in a new direction, and he did not know how to express his fears, except with anger.

However, this stain on my long-awaited graduation day is not my only memory: I remember my brother and Uncle Anton flying in to see me walk across the stage. I remember perfect San Diego weather—a crisp blue sky and cheerful sunlight drenching the crowd of graduates and our families and friends. I remember hearing Tata's voice as my name was being announced through a microphone. I remember walking with my chin held high and feeling Tata's presence with me as I approached the dean. I could feel Tata's loving hands and feel her beaming pride as the dean handed me my *real* diploma and we shook hands. Even today, when I close my eyes and think about the day I officially became the first formally educated woman in my family, my memory is flooded with intense, bright, joyous sunlight.

Shortly after I graduated, Malek and I had a fight that was a defining moment in our marriage. I don't remember what caused the argument, but I remember that we were in the living room screaming at each other. He rushed heatedly into the kitchen that faced our living room and shouted, "I'm going to take all of our dishes, throw them on the floor, and break them!"

I looked at him, his energy like clouds of smoke coming out of a train engine, and I thought of my father and the hundreds of times I'd seen him smash glasses, picture frames, and crystal. At that moment, I refused to feel terrified the way I had as a girl in my father's home.

My adrenaline was flowing, but I walked calmly into the kitchen and stood no more than a foot away from Malek. I didn't care how much anger was spewing out of him. I opened the closest cabinet door and turned to him. "You want to break everything?" I asked. Then I looked directly into his eyes. "Go ahead," I said.

Malek turned his face away from mine, fuming. He walked back to the living room and sat in his chair. He picked up the remote and turned the television on, as he always did at the end of a fight.

A couple of weeks later, I traveled to Jordan. There, my family showered me with gifts of money, and I used some of it to buy myself a graduation gift. I visited Silsal, a store that sells unique ceramics; it is known for selling objects that are traditionally crafted and have traditional styles mixed with modern techniques and designs. I purchased a simple but striking ceramic bowl. It was flat-finished, off-white, and etched with simple, traditional engravings of black animals that encircle the bowl. When I returned to the States, I displayed the bowl on our coffee table. It became a symbol and daily reminder of my accomplishment.

I also began applying for jobs. In October, Merrill Lynch selected me to join an entry-level financial adviser training program. Getting this job meant that I did start earning money. A month after I started, I purchased a brand-new 2000 Volkswagen Golf. Out of excitement for my new accomplishments, I insisted on putting the car in my name alone, though Malek wanted me to put it in his name. When I refused, he suggested that I put it in both of our names. But I insisted on putting the car in my name alone; I wanted to feel that I owned one thing.

As I started building my confidence and rising, Malek started shrinking. His jewelry business wasn't doing as well in the States as he had hoped it would. There was a lot of competition, so it was difficult to penetrate the market. He transferred whatever positive balances he had into an account in Jordan. As I started earning income, he became open to the idea of my contributing to pay our expenses, and I did. But my salary was not enough to support us fully, so we started accruing debt.

Even with the new debts, I was excited about my educational and professional growth. For Malek's birthday, I bought him a brown leather wallet and made a 6:00 p.m. reservation at Benihana, a Japanese steakhouse. For a change, I wanted to treat him. I didn't tell him the details; he only knew I was planning a surprise and that he needed to be home by five o'clock.

I had shared my plans with my mother-in-law earlier in the week. "Amto Kasma, I haven't told him anything. I'm going to surprise him," I said. I imagined she would be pleased that her daughter-in-law wanted to do something nice for her son.

On his birthday, Malek called me at work around 2:00 p.m. and said, "My mother just called. My parents want to come over to our apartment this evening for my birthday." I was shocked once again, though I should not have been.

I called my mother-in-law and reminded her that I had a surprise dinner planned for Malek. I invited her to visit us over the weekend instead. She acted innocent on the phone, as if she'd simply forgotten. "Tayyeb ya binti," she told me. Okay, my daughter.

Less than ten minutes after I hung up with her, Malek called back. "What have you done?" he asked, exhaling smoke with frustration. "My mother now thinks that she is not welcome in our apartment, and she is offended. You need to find a way to fix this."

She hadn't told him the plans explicitly, but the surprise was ruined. I had to cancel the reservation. Malek's birthday celebration began with him feeling angry and believing that I had offended his mother. We hosted his parents at our apartment that night, and they left satisfied. He was happy as well, for having pleased his parents. Not believing what had happened that day, I went to bed in tears.

One Saturday, after some time had passed between my graduation and his birthday, I said, "I'm noticing that the people who are getting promotions are the ones who have a master's degree. Now that I've graduated, I would like to research areas of study for my master's." I hoped my comment would open up a conversation.

Malek's response was immediate. He didn't answer, "Let's think about the possibilities," or ask, "How could we make it work with a family?" Instead, he said firmly and simply, "No. You're not going to complete your master's. A bachelor's is enough. It's time for you to have children, to become a mother, and to take care of them and me." He picked up his cigarettes and lit one. I knew that this was the only conversation we would have on the topic. He expected me to have no aspirations for personal and professional growth; I had no control for making decisions about my own life and no hope that I ever would.

It was becoming clear to me that we approached life differently now. When our families had first introduced us, we seemed to be the right fit—perfect for each other. The practical reasons by which we had seemed to be a good fit created a nice frame, but the picture inside did not match. Many people would shut up and accept a nice frame, but I couldn't. I'd come to the United States, and I had changed. Malek had not. At nineteen, I possessed a dif-

ferent worldview than I did at twenty-four. I could not ignore my
emerging identity.

After I returned from Jordan, we attended the wedding of a family friend. The father of the groom was also a Jordanian jeweler.
His business in the States was successful, and the man was quite
wealthy. Malek considered him a mentor, and in fact, years before we were married, Malek had worked for and learned from
him. Later, when Malek opened his own business in San Diego,
he was looking for creative ways to partner with this man, but it
never came to fruition.

The wedding was at the Immaculata Catholic Church at the
University of San Diego, a private Catholic university. I hadn't
been inside a Catholic church since I'd left Jordan, and the moment we arrived, I was overcome with awe. The church, which sat
atop a hill that overlooked the ocean, was completely stunning.
The white exterior entry was ornately carved around an arched
entryway made up of two giant wooden doors. A carved statue of
the Virgin Mary was in a recessed area above this entry. The bell
tower that seemed to rise up like a bright, white vine against the
blue sky was topped with a dome covered in aqua tiles, with gold
trim delineating segments around the dome. On top of another
dome, there was a statue of a saint. The architecture reminded
me of a mixture of Spanish and Middle Eastern styles. Inside, I
found a blue ceiling and stained glass that illuminated the entire
church. The sides were lined with small chapels, each dedicated
to a different saint.

A tiny voice in my heart said, *If I ever get to do my master's,
this is where I want to go.* I didn't know anything about the uni-

versity, but I fell in love with the church and campus; they seemed to hold beauty and positive energy. I knew I wasn't allowed to pursue a master's. Malek had already said "no," and I knew his decision was firm. So regardless of that little voice, it was a dream that was unreachable. The expectations for the way I was to live came into direct opposition with how I wanted to live. I was not just battling to discover myself within the confines and expectations of the Middle Eastern community, but I was also struggling to exist in the larger American community to which my Middle Eastern ties would not permit me to belong. I was stuck between two cultures—lost, with no clear sense of self.

One day, after Malek came home from visiting his parents' house, he seemed shaken. Gently, he took my wrist and led me to our bedroom. We sat beside each other on the edge of our bed. He said, "My family and I decided that it is best for us to return to Jordan to reestablish our business there."

I knew immediately that he was devastated; he had always wanted to live and retire in the States. He was not able to hold back his tears. I watched them drip down his pale cheeks. I had never seen Malek so ashamed and disappointed in himself.

After he finished relaying the plans, he looked closely into my eyes and asked, "Are you supporting me in this decision?"

I held him and said, "Of course I am. We are in this together." He seemed almost desperate to have my approval. It is one of the only times I remember him opening up to me as an equal partner. For me, being partners was a welcomed experience, something I had longed for throughout our entire marriage; for him, it was probably emasculating.

19) *The Saving Graces*

In May 2000, Malek returned to Jordan to reestablish his business there. With this distance and time apart, I saw clearly that our marriage was deteriorating. I wasn't happy. On the one hand, I had taken steps forward when I finished my bachelor's and started working in an entry-level job with Merrill Lynch. On the other hand, I had regressed. Malek had insisted that he would not want me to be on my own while he was in Jordan. I moved out of our apartment and moved in with Malek's parents, his brother and sister-in-law, and their son. While Malek was back to Jordan to get his business under way, I was working and contributing to the household expenses in my new "group living" situation while also paying down our debt.

I had my own bedroom and shared a bathroom with Malek's brother and his wife and their two-year-old son. In addition to living in a crowded house, every afternoon, Malek's sister, who lived a few minutes away, stopped over to visit with her six-year-old son. In these tight quarters, there was little privacy. My mother-in-law used to stand behind the bedroom door while I was on the phone. Or during the twenty-minute weekly call I was allowed to make to my parents and to Malek on Saturdays, she would pick up the other line to listen in. When the conversations didn't reveal anything interesting to her, I would hear a gentle *click*.

I had no real say in my life; this period gave me a glimpse of the future waiting for me in Jordan. I could envision my father and Malek picking up where they left off in their power struggle over me, and I knew my life would be worse there. Yet I was tormented even imagining the consequences of leaving my husband. I thought the repercussions would be unbearable. I thought that I was stuck, that my life was over, and there was no chance for a better life.

During my weekly calls with Malek, we discussed our debts and his business losses. He had begun to open up about these subjects now that he needed my modest income. Otherwise, we had little else to share with each other. I started dreading Fridays, because I knew that on Saturdays I would have to speak to him. Twenty minutes speaking to my mother or sister seemed to pass in an instant, but these calls with Malek felt long.

One Saturday, I told Malek, "Merrill Lynch has opened a new office in Jordan. I might be able to transfer my position to the office there. If I do, I might even get the opportunity to travel for work, since there are so few offices in the region." I wanted to see how he would react, whether he would be supportive of this opportunity.

I could hear him smoking, taking forceful drags. "You need to realize," he told me, with anger oozing through his words, "that once you move back home to Jordan, it's time for you to have children and stay home."

For the first time, I began to question the pure perfect vase and every other lesson I had been taught about my identity as a Middle Eastern woman. I dared to question the norms that were made to silence women. My questioning brought a surge of indignation. This conflict drove me to open my eyes and admit to myself how unhappy I was and how disconnected I felt from Malek.

As I started becoming aware of the vast differences between Malek and me, I felt uncomfortable about having children with him. His father had bragged about not seeing his three children often when they were growing up. Amo Dawoud had invested financially in his children's education, but he hadn't been involved in their day-to-day upbringing.

I had asked Malek once, "If we had a child, would you help out? For instance, would you change our baby's diapers?"

He answered, "No. I'm not going to wipe my son's butt. That's your responsibility."

His attitude was fixed about many things; being set in his ways about parenting before we had even become parents made me uneasy about having children together. I wanted my children to have a father who would be engaged and involved in their lives.

Thankfully, Malek's struggling business gave us another reason to wait, and we agreed to postpone having children for one more year when we thought we would be back on our feet. By the end of that year, Malek had moved to Jordan. While I wasn't happy about our circumstances, I was relieved that we would wait even longer.

I continued to question my identity and purpose, but I could not find a meaningful answer. As each year passed, the road became narrower and darker. After four years of marriage, I found myself at a dead-end. I was twenty-four, and I was suffocating in my own despair. I could no longer see any glimmer of hope for my life to improve. I felt empty, unhappy, and lost, all while idly sitting in a life without light.

In my darkness, I heard a woman's voice whisper from within: *Dima, you weren't meant for this life. Don't accept this. You are worth so much more. Leave.* Was it Tata? Was it my own inner voice? Was it just a fantasy? Too afraid to crack my vase, I silenced the thought of freedom and the desire for self-worth. That life would not be permitted or accepted by my family in San Diego or by my family in Jordan.

In November, Malek had been away for nearly six months. That month, I woke up early one rainy Saturday and drove to my office, knowing there would be only one or two people working. I knew I would have more privacy there than I would at home. I went into a conference room, closed the door, and dialed my calling card number into my cell phone before dialing my family's number in Jordan. There were no windows in the room, so I stared at the image of the Merrill Lynch bull framed and hung on the wall. My father and sister were not home, and I was happy to get to talk with my mother alone. I began opening up about my unhappiness.

My mother was accustomed to hearing women in our family and community, including herself, say that they were unhappy. But this was always a mere complaint; the women always ended up staying in their marriages. In most cases, women my age got pregnant with a first or second or third child. They became busy raising their children and blocked out the sense of misery they felt.

"Once you move back to Jordan and live with your husband again, you'll get pregnant," my mom told me. "Things will work themselves out with you and Malek, and you will be happy."

I closed my eyes and took a deep breath. I could feel my heart pounding as I found my courage and opened my mouth. Then, I dared to breathe the words, "I want to leave my marriage."

"No," she immediately responded. "Don't even think about it. Do you understand the consequences of this decision? If you leave, you will ruin our family." My mother was unyielding. "It is not an option."

I was desperate for support, but instead of receiving support, I was reminded that breaking my vase meant walking on the sharp and painful shards of its remains. These warnings fed my fears.

When we hung up, I cried with a total sense of helplessness. Then I calmed myself down, dried my eyes, walked through the rain to my car, and drove home.

One morning in March 2001, while Malek was still in Jordan, I woke just before sunrise and lay there, in my bed, in my in-laws' home. For months, I had been consumed with confusion, fear, and deep depression. That morning, my mind and body were too numb to do anything but stare at the ceiling. I stayed in bed for hours, paralyzed, staring at nothing.

I was living inside a golden cage: shiny and beautiful externally, but behind the gilded bars, restrictive and empty. I could not stay confined by these bars, but I could not fly out either. I was stuck, and I knew I needed guidance. By late morning, I got the energy to get out of bed and pick up the phone. I called my mother in Jordan, but she wasn't home. I called my best friend Bana in Jordan, but I couldn't get her either. With my last shred of hope, I called Uncle Anton in New Mexico, but he didn't answer. I yearned for counsel from the people that I trusted, but no one was around.

I was not even twenty-five years old, and I felt that my life was over. There was nothing to live for. I was desperate to hear any hint of hope that life could get better. I was at my lowest point, more emotionally disconnected from Malek than ever, and deeply unhappy with the person I was becoming by trying to satisfy him and his family's expectations. I could not recognize myself.

Yet—even though I did not want to feel like his property, even though we fought, and even though I felt distanced from him— Malek was the man I loved. So, out of desperation I called my husband in the middle of the week; it must have been eleven or twelve in the afternoon in San Diego and evening in Jordan. For once, I could not wait until our Saturday-morning call.

His workday had ended, and he'd just come from dinner with a friend. I said, "Malek, I am not okay. I think I am depressed, and I don't know what to do."

He didn't respond right away. I could hear the last *Athan* filtering into the house through open windows. I needed his assurance, and if he could give that to me, I would have a sign that there was a chance for us. I hoped to hear him say, "Things will work out *habibti*, my love. It is all going to be okay."

Instead, I heard dry, harsh words: "Who do you think you are?" he asked. "Fucking Princess Diana?"

I held my breath as I listened to him light a cigarette, the lighter clicking under his thumb. I couldn't respond.

"What do you mean you're depressed?" he continued. "Come see the women here, how abused and silenced they are. You have a better life, and you are complaining?"

When we hung up, tears streamed down my cheeks; my chest became heavy. That weight pulled me to the floor. I felt deflated, as if the ground had cracked open beneath me. I sobbed uncontrollably and out loud. I had rarely prayed during my marriage, but I was desperate. I stayed on the ground crying and begging, "Please, God, help me. Please, tell me what to do."

The whispering voice, the one that had told me I was not meant for this life, came back; this time it was louder and firmer than before. Maybe it had been rising to the surface slowly over time; maybe it was awakened while I was sitting on the carpet in the bedroom experiencing the lowest point of my life, holding the phone, crying, and begging for help; maybe a tiny sliver of the early-spring sunshine found its way through a crack in the closed blinds and shone on my skin. I don't know from where exactly it originated, but somewhere within, I could hear a voice in my head. *Leave*, it said. When I heard it, I cried harder.

Hours passed. My eyes were raw from crying. Every time I thought of staying in that marriage, I saw a dense black future. I realized that my life was not going to get better, but only worse, with more expectations and restrictions after I moved back to Jordan.

The fear of continuing to lose myself overshadowed the fear of leaving. For the very first time in my life, I realized that I *did* have a choice, regardless of the risks and uncertainty involved: I could choose to stay and continue to satisfy everyone around me, continue to be quietly miserable, or I could choose to leave and give myself permission to start a new life. I knew I needed to listen to the counsel of that whisper, the counsel of my intuition. I knew I needed to leave.

Looking back, I'm grateful that Malek was the only person I could reach on the telephone that day. His words helped me make a clear choice; his words forced me to listen to my own voice.

Just beyond the fifteen-mile radius of my Little Middle East— both at San Diego State University and also at Merrill Lynch— I could see and taste the life I was meant to live; it was right in front of me. But the path to that life held potentially deadly consequences. Every woman in my life had been too terrified of these consequences. But for me, at that exact moment, shattering my perfect vase was the only option. This decision was the real saving grace.

20 Resurrection

Imagine the sound of a telephone constantly ringing; imagine hundreds and hundreds of calls transpiring. My new life played out in a series of telephone calls. Sometimes I was the caller, and sometimes I was the recipient. The sound of a phone ringing, whether outgoing or incoming, became like my heartbeat. It was the sound of connection to life, but it could easily have been the sound of death. If the words to be spoken over the line might stop my heart from beating, I prayed in advance that I would be resurrected.

In the spring of 2001, in April alone, I spent more than five hundred dollars buying minutes on calling cards. They began with a call to my father.

I found the courage to share my broken marriage with my father. I didn't know if he would support me, but I knew I had no other choice. "I can't stay married to Malek anymore; I have to leave," I told him, and I explained the reasons. He listened in silence on the other end of the telephone, and with each sentence that left my mouth, I felt like I shed another layer of my suffering. When I was finished, I waited, prepared to hear his disappointment, and possibly his anger.

To my shock, he responded, "I will not allow Malek and his family to continue to treat you with disrespect. Leave him. You have my support."

I had always wondered what it felt like to have a father who was on my side, protecting me unconditionally. I'd felt a glimmer of this when I was in high school, and he shepherded me through my exams. That day, connected only through the telephone line, I felt that protection in full force. It was one of the few times in my life that I experienced being a daughter whose father fully supported and protected her. The surge of love I felt for my father at that moment filled me like a wave and gave me the power I needed to move forward.

I leased an apartment in an older, low-income neighborhood in Poway. I didn't spend a lot of time searching for the perfect location or the perfect apartment. I took what I could find quickly and for little money. The apartment was not in the safest area, but it was on the second floor and faced a small pool. Being close to the water was one minor, soothing comfort. My budget was tight. A salary of thirty thousand dollars did not go far in San Diego, and out of mine, I would pay $820 in monthly rent, the cost of utilities, food, a car note, car insurance, a home phone bill, a cell phone bill, and personal expenses. I felt overwhelmed financially, and I wasn't sure how I would survive. I just knew it would be better than the life I'd been living. This was my first step to freedom.

The first thing I did was to go to the bank, where Malek and I shared a safe deposit box that contained my gold. I took the jewelry out and opened a safe deposit box in another bank that was under my name, alone. I also rented a small storage space. Over the next two weeks, I moved my possessions out of my in-laws' home. In preparation for my move back to Jordan, over the last year, I'd been buying new clothes, bath mats, nice toiletries—typical American items that I found on sale and knew would feel like luxuries in Amman. On rare mornings or evenings when all of my in-laws were occupied, I took these things to the unit. I also kept photo albums and trinkets with sentimental value, including the bowl I'd purchased for myself in Jordan as a graduation gift.

Easter was approaching in San Diego. I would drive under clear blue skies past nice, large suburban homes decorated with pastel Easter egg wreaths and bunny rabbit statues into an industrial park with nondescript streets and nondescript metal buildings rising at their edges. I would park my car, turn off the engine, get out, and open the storage door. My last trip there, I sat on the concrete and faced the open unit. I stared at the boxes in front of me. They were stuffed with memories I could not handle. After a long time, I stood up, rolled the heavy door down, locked it, walked to my car, and drove away. I couldn't go back for over a year.

During this period, I spoke to my parents several times to let them know how things were progressing and to let them know that I was okay. Baba paid for a plane ticket for my brother to fly from New Mexico to San Diego to be with me on the day I moved out. He wanted Waseem to be by my side; with my brother there, by extension, my father was also there to protect me.

On April 15, 2001, Malek's family had plans to celebrate Easter Sunday at his aunt's house. Christmas Eve was *always* at Malek's sister's home. Christmas Day was *always* at Malek's parents' home. Thanksgiving was *always* at the home of Malek's sister's mother-in-law. And Easter was *always* at his aunt's house. These traditions were fixed.

I made up a lie that I'd been invited to spend Easter with some coworkers, though I knew this would not go over well. My mother-in-law was disappointed in me and told me so multiple

times that morning. "You should be with family on Easter." I
knew my absence would embarrass her. My father-in-law did not
hold back his judgment either. He spent the morning mumbling
angry words under his breath every time he walked down the
hallway past my room. I caught the words "disrespectful," "un-
grateful," "insulting," and "shameful." The voices of old ladies
and old men from my childhood came back to me. "Aib, Dima.
Aib," I could hear them saying.

This was the day I would move out, the day I'd been waiting
for, and that was all that mattered to me.

When my parents-in-law and Malek's brother's family finally
closed the garage door behind them, I exhaled with a mix of relief
and panic. I could feel my adrenaline pumping as I picked up my
cell phone to call Waseem. "They're gone," I told him. "I'll come
pick you up in a few minutes."

He was staying at a La Quinta Inn in Poway, less than fifteen
minutes away from Malek's parents' house and ten minutes west
of the apartment I had rented two weeks earlier. When we got
back to their house, Waseem helped me carry my clothes on their
hangers and some folded items to the car. He slammed the trunk
down hard, and when I heard it, I wished it could be as easy to
shut out the life I was leaving.

As Waseem pulled away, I looked straight ahead. I didn't care
what was to my left or my right. Moving forward was all that
mattered. I was terrified and did not know what to expect, but I
knew my life would never be the same again.

Sitting in the passenger seat, I made three calls. First, I called
my parents. "I am safe and out of the house," I told my father. He
asked to talk to Waseem and instructed him again to take good
care of me.

Second, I called my mother-in-law. "I am no longer in your
house," I told her. "I left. I'm out of the house for good, and I'm
not coming back." My adrenaline was still pumping, and I was

terrified, but delivering those words, I also felt a sense of power that was completely unfamiliar.

"What do you mean you are out?" she gasped. "What are you talking about?" First she sounded angry and shocked. Then she sounded panicked, "Aah, aah. My blood pressure," she started moaning.

I could picture her tilting her head back and waving her hands in front of her face to get air, as I had seen her do every time she was unhappy with a situation. Usually, this was a way for her to get attention or to get her way. Every time, the second after she got what she wanted, she looked and acted completely normal. On this day, I believed that, for once, her blood pressure actually had shot up.

I could hear my father-in-law's voice and Malek's aunt in the background asking, "What is going on? What is happening?"

"Congratulations," I told Amto Kasma. "You just destroyed your son's and my marriage." I knew this was only partly true, but I'd spent years restraining my frustration with her meddling. In that moment, it felt good to be bold.

The third call I made that afternoon was to Malek, but his line was busy. At the time, there was no call waiting or voicemail in Jordan. After we arrived at the apartment, I kept redialing the number over the next half hour, but I couldn't get through. I guessed that his mother had gotten to him first, pouring the news out to her son.

Forty-five minutes after I'd first hung up with my mother-in-law, my cell phone rang. The number on the screen was an international number. I answered, "Hello?"

"Dima, I just hung up from a call with my mother," Malek said, breathing heavily. "What the hell have you done?" Without waiting for a response, he screamed, "Are you cheating on me? Are you on drugs?"

I was shocked that he was imagining such outrageous scenarios. Then I realized that he just couldn't fathom the simple truth—that I wasn't happy in our marriage; this reality was inconceivable to him.

I managed to remain composed for the duration of the call, which lasted only a few minutes. I tried to speak calmly, telling him that I was finally done and I was sorry things were this way.

But he wouldn't stop to hear what I was saying. He continued screaming into the phone.

Finally, I said, "Malek, I am not coming back, and I'm going to hang up now." Then, I did. I looked at Waseem. Having him there in the room with me was a source of strength.

The next day, I drove Waseem to the airport. From that point forward, I made daily calls to my parents to update them and assure them I was safe. During those calls, my father told me how worried he was about me being alone for the first time in my life. He told me he was trying his best to take care of me from the other side of the world. My father told me repeatedly, "Dima, I am on your side."

Each time I heard those words, I felt loved and protected all over again. Without those words, I might have crumbled under this enormous act of defiance. When I think back to how this made me feel, an image sweeps through my mind: my father walking his daughter through the snow.

A week after I moved out, Uncle Anton called from New Mexico. He said, "Dima, be careful. I have a feeling that your in-laws will start following you on your way to and from work, and they may even hire a private investigator." My uncle had always had good intuition, but this time I did not believe him. I didn't believe that the situation would get that bad.

The next day, while I was driving home from work, I found

myself stuck in rush-hour traffic, in a sea of honking cars and ex-
haust fumes. After a while, I realized that a navy Honda minivan was trailing me. I do not remember where I was when I first
saw it appear, but a few minutes into my commute, I'd seen it turn
left when I turned left. Once the traffic was moving again, I noticed the same minivan and realized that again, it turned right
when I turned right. It slowed down and sped up when I did. I
was not convinced that the car was following me, so I began driving on narrow side roads. That's when it became obvious and
undeniable.

With the van trailing behind me, I drove to a neighborhood in
Poway that had an old, defunct train station; it was used only on
the weekend for children's activities. I pulled into the parking lot
and parked in one of the many empty spaces. The minivan pulled
in behind me and parked to my right. There were no other cars
around. I looked out of the passenger window at the driver and
saw a woman with blonde hair and pale skin. She appeared to be
American, and I had never seen her before. I couldn't see if there
were other people in the car with her. It felt like we were daring
each other to make the next move. I did not have the guts to step
out of the car. The woman also continued sitting in the driver's
seat. She stared straight ahead without looking at me.

After a few minutes, I put my car in reverse and peeled out of
the empty parking lot. Through my rearview mirror, I kept my
eyes on the minivan. It stayed parked there, getting smaller and
smaller until it was a speck in the distance.

When I was safely back in my apartment, I sat on the carpet next
to the phone. I called Uncle Anton. I told him what happened and
asked him to stay on the line with me until I could breathe at a
normal rate again.

At last, I said, "What have I done? Maybe it was a mistake."

"Dima, don't look back," he said calmly. "Do you hear me?"

"I hear you," I answered, my voice wavering.

"Don't think of going back to Malek. Just move forward with your life. Just move on."

"Okay," I said. "Okay . . ."

"Do you need me to come to San Diego?" he offered. "I can arrange for some time off."

"No," I said, firmly. "I'll be okay. Baba bought a ticket for Auntie Nadia to fly in from Toronto to stay with me for a month," I told him. "She'll be here in a few days. And a week after that, at the beginning of May, Mama will also be here for ten days."

When he heard that my mother would be arriving soon, he cautioned, "Be careful, Dima. Your mom is going to be like a black angel."

I felt confused. "What do you mean?" I asked.

"I mean, she will *act* like an angel, like your savior. But in reality, she is conditioned to create self-doubt."

As soon as he said this, I understood. He was worried she would plant seeds of doubt, tell me the negative things people in our community in Amman had been saying, and cause me to question whether I had made the right decision.

"I will be careful." I added, "I won't change my mind. I know this is the right thing." I wasn't fully convinced this was true, and he must have detected my feelings.

"Don't look back," he repeated. Then he said, "Promise yourself."

"I promise," I told him.

When the first week of May rolled around, I had been on my own for three weeks. It felt like a lifetime. Early one morning, around

7:00 a.m., I was at work, staring at my computer screen. I was watching the stock tickers blinking green and red, but I was too distracted to really read the stock symbols. I could only comprehend the changing colors—green with stocks going up, red with stocks going down.

My office phone rang. "I am in San Diego," Malek said after I answered. He was speaking in a calm and loving voice. "I landed at 10:00 p.m. last night, and I am here to see you. I want to make our marriage work. And I want to take you with me to Jordan." He continued, "I'm staying at a hotel in Rancho Bernardo. My parents do not know that I am in town. They would not approve if I told them that I am trying to get back together with you. They're upset and do not want you to be part of our family anymore. This is going to be a tough situation, but *I* want you back."

My heart pounded, and my stomach turned with a mix of joyful and fearful nerves.

"Have lunch with me today," he said. "Let's talk in person."

"I don't know. I want to think about it," I told him. As soon as we hung up, I called my mother at my apartment. When I told her what had happened, I could hear that she was excited.

"Go," she told me. "Go and meet with him. See what he has to say." It had been almost a full year since he'd left to work on his business in Jordan. I thought it could be good to see each other face-to-face. Like my mother, there was a part of me that felt excited, and I wondered if seeing him in person would change the way I felt about my decision.

I picked up the phone and called Malek back. "Okay," I said. "I'll see you. Where do you want to meet?" Malek picked one of our favorite places, a Mexican restaurant less than five minutes from my office, and one we had been to together many times before he left for Jordan.

I parked my car and started walking up to the main entrance, where he was waiting. He was wearing blue jeans and a white button-down shirt. He saw me right away, and we locked eyes.

He looked pale and sad. But as he watched me walking toward him, his face lifted.

My heart started beating quickly as I got closer to him. I felt happy to see him and also terrified, knowing that there was a chance that I would give myself back to him. When I was standing in front of Malek, it didn't matter that we were near a crowded parking lot and facing a busy street, and nothing that had transpired between us in the last years mattered. We hugged and kissed each other openly and passionately.

When we pulled apart from each other, we walked into the restaurant holding each other's hand; this felt safe and comforting, and I remembered how much I had missed him.

When the waitress came to take our order, Malek ordered for both of us. This was something he had never done before, and it was strange. Even stranger was that he'd forgotten that I am a vegetarian. He ordered chicken quesadillas and beef fajitas, both items I could not eat. I ignored this oversight, trying to stay focused on the reason for our reunion—to discuss our marriage and figure out if there was something we could do to save it.

Malek started talking as soon as the waitress left the table. "I have so much to tell you," he began. "I have been seeing a counselor, Dima. I remember that you told me that we should go to a marriage counselor. When you left me, I realized that you were right."

I felt pleased that he had sought out help and was trying to make our marriage work. This gave me a glimmer of hope; I sat quietly listening to him.

"The bishop who married us is counseling me," he said. "He has made it clear to me why you left. He told me that a woman's castle is her home. He said that since I asked you to give up our home and live with my parents while I was in Jordan, you felt that you lost your castle and this, as a result, is what caused you to leave me."

The first thought that came to my mind was that this bishop had no clue what he was talking about. I did not leave Malek because my castle had been taken away from me. The issues that pushed me away were the lack of respect and communication, the suffocating expectations, the lack of appreciation, Malek's selfishness and judgments, and the way he and his family wanted to control me. I realized at that moment that Malek did not understand how disconnected we were, and I was overcome with sadness.

As I processed my emotions, Malek kept talking. "I'm having furniture custom-built for our new home in Jordan. Last month, I hired a carpenter to design and build our bedroom and dining room." Excitedly, he pulled out a picture from his pocket and began showing me the furniture he had already chosen for us.

I looked at the photo and saw that it was a light-colored wood, my least favorite finish. The design was nothing that I would have picked, but I knew he expected me to accept his choice and act happy. I looked at the animated way Malek was speaking and thought, *I would have liked for us to pick our furniture together, but we have more critical issues to figure out. I'm going to keep listening.*

Malek looked at me, waiting to see some excitement, but I just nodded. He didn't get the reaction that he was hoping for. Trying to brush aside his displeasure, he set the paper down on the table and pulled one more item from his pocket. Suddenly, he was holding a box in his right hand. He removed the lid, reached across the table, and placed both of my hands into his left hand. In his right hand, he was holding a gold ring, sparkling with several diamond baguettes.

I recognized it as one of the newest and most expensive designs in his catalog. Before I knew what was happening—before I could comprehend the waves of joy and sadness washing through my body at turns, Malek was putting the ring on my empty ring finger. He seemed unfazed by my missing wedding ring. "Dima," he said, still holding my hand in his, "I want you to come back with me to Jordan."

A mix of fear, excitement, and joy all rose up inside me. I looked at him with tears welling in my eyes, and when he saw this, his lips turned up into a soft smile. He took my tears as an answer.

But before I could actually speak, he continued, "But I have to share with you that my parents are very disappointed in you. They do not want you to be part of our family. I will have to find a way to convince them to accept you again. I intentionally did not tell them that I was coming to town; I did not want to hear their discouraging opinion about me trying to get you back."

There it was—a clear indication that he would always put his family's expectations ahead of our relationship. I believed then, and I believe now, that he is a good man. But this lunch confirmed that I could not go back.

The waitress returned to the table with a large, round, black tray filled with our food. She placed the dishes in the middle of the table and set an empty plate in front of each of us.

Malek gestured at the food and waited for me to fill my plate. "Kuli, kuli," he said—eat, eat—waving his hands over the plates.

"I can't eat any of this," I told him. I felt both crushed and calm as I spoke. "Don't you remember that I am a vegetarian?" I could see that he remembered immediately and felt embarrassed. "Don't worry," I said. "You go ahead and eat."

Still embarrassed, Malek started filling his plate. Then his mood shifted. As he began eating, his temper changed. He said, his voice now hardened, "Let me make things simple for you. You either fly with me back to Jordan by the end of this week, quietly, with no resistance, or I will request you under *Biet at Ta'ah*."

I was instantly thrown back into my childhood. I could feel myself, a six-year-old girl with eyes glued to the television, staring intently while a thick-bearded man on the screen threatened to force his estranged wife to return to him in the name of *Biet at Ta'ah*, the law that allowed men to drag their wives back to them. I felt my heart thumping behind my chest.

Sitting there in the restaurant, I was a twenty-four-year-old woman and also a young child trying to decipher fact from fiction, asking myself whether the man in front of me was serious. I tried to process what I was hearing. *But we are Christians*, I told myself. *He would not dare use this law to enforce our marriage.* I reminded myself: *I am in America;* Biet at Ta'ah *does not apply here. It cannot. Can it?*

His lunch invitation, the hugs and kisses, the nice words, and the diamond ring were all empty gestures. In a flash, I imagined what my life in Jordan would be if I went back to him; I knew immediately that it would be impossible. I took a breath, I put the ring in front of him on the table, and I said, "I am not going back with you."

I stood up and walked out of the restaurant alone. I walked to my car, got in, and drove to my office, still shaking.

A few days later, Malek flew back to Jordan alone.

When I told my father about the *Beit at Ta'ah* threat, he erupted in anger. "I am going to teach him a lesson," he shouted through the phone. "I will teach him and his family a lesson!" I was reminded of his eruption after my engagement party. I felt supported, but that memory made me feel sick at the same time.

I knew my father was well connected with officials in the government and could easily cause harm to Malek without major repercussions.

I begged him not to do anything. "The situation is bad enough,"

I said. "I do not want things to get worse." My father promised that he would not do anything to harm Malek, and I trusted him.

Around the third week of May, Malek called my office around 11:00 a.m. my time and 9:00 p.m. his time. I was placing stock trades for clients according to my manager Jessica's instructions when I saw his number on the caller ID. I transferred the call to voicemail. I needed to concentrate to avoid making mistakes. Four or five minutes later, the phone rang again, and again I transferred the call to voicemail. This continued, on and on, with the international number reappearing on the caller ID.

Once I completed the stock trades, I checked my voicemail. There were five messages from Malek.

In the first, he was upset, and he sounded drunk. "You fucking bitch," he growled. "Who do you think you are to leave me?" In the next breath, he said, "Your father—how dare he humiliate me? I know he tipped off the airport customs that I was smuggling diamonds and gold without claiming them. Customs held me for over three hours, searching me again and again." He laughed bitterly. "They found nothing! But I knew immediately that your father caused that mess. When you move back to Jordan, you will not speak with your parents or even visit them. I never want to see him or talk with him again."

In the second voicemail, he said, "I love you, Dima. I am so sorry for what I said and did. Please forgive me and come back. Please come back."

In the third, he said, "You will never survive on your own. You will soon call me begging like a dog for me to take you back. Then I will be kind and will take you back."

In the fourth, he said, "Dima, *habibti*, my love, come back to me."

Finally, in the last message, I heard, "You are nothing but a bitch. You embarrassed my parents and me. I will never forgive you."

My ears were completely tuned into the headset as I listened to the voicemails, one after the other. With every message I listened to, it felt like a part of me was dying. It was one thing to leave him. It was another to hear the man I loved scream such cruel words in my direction. My tears dropped; and at the same time, I was unable to move or even blink. I was not even sure if I was breathing. I stared at the black phone with my finger clicking the number "3" after the end of each message, in order to hear the next message.

I shifted my gaze from the phone to a framed affirmation written by Walter D. Wintle. I had bought it at a Hallmark store and recently hung it on my cubicle wall to the right side of my computer screen. I replayed the messages, but now, instead of listening, I found myself reading the affirmation. Even after I hung up the phone, I sat there rereading the words.

If you think you are beaten, you are
If you think you dare not, you don't,
If you like to win, but you think you can't
It is almost certain you won't.

If you think you'll lose, you're lost.
For out of the world we find,
Success begins with a fellow's will
It's all in the state of mind.

If you think you are outclassed, you are
You've got to think high to rise,
You've got to be sure of yourself before
You can ever win the prize.

Life's battles don't always go
To the stronger or faster man,
But soon or late the man who wins
Is the man WHO THINKS HE CAN!

I don't know how long I spent reading these words, but I had
no energy to do anything else except read. Each time I got to one
line, it seemed to glare like headlights in my eyes: "You've got to
think high to rise."

PART THREE

All the
Beautiful
Shards

21 ⟩ Life in the Movies

There is the life we are living, and there is the life we imagine living. After my mother went back to Jordan and Auntie Nadia went back to Canada at the end of May, I was determined to fend for myself. My job at Merrill Lynch was a lifeline, but at the same time, I was making barely enough to survive. With the break from my old life, I wanted to discover how I fit into and belonged in this world, not just merely how to survive. There was one problem: I was completely stripped of my self-confidence and self-worth.

If I wanted to discover my place in the world, I needed to make a major shift in how I viewed my story. I needed to alter my self-perception and no longer think of myself as a young girl filled with fears and haunted by expectations. I needed to distinguish myself as a new woman: self-empowered, confident, and responsible for her own choices.

But here is the life I was living: I was terrified about my finances, I cried daily, and I searched for anything I could take comfort in. To keep myself occupied and calm on the weekends, I went to the Savon Pharmacy on Saturdays and spent over an hour in the makeup aisle. It was meditative to me. I felt safe there and distracted from reality by the colorful products and the possibilities they seemed to promise. In an attempt for companionship, I bought a fish tank and ten tiny, colorful fish. Two weeks after I got them, I cleaned the tank and replaced the water, without realizing that the fish would not be able to acclimate to new water. The next morning, all the fish were floating dead.

My apartment had few items, less than the necessities. In the bedroom, there was a new mattress with a bare metal frame, an aqua-colored bed cover, and my clothes hanging in a small closet. In the kitchen, I had one pot, one pan, a big blue mug, and a few other disposable items, just enough to boil a pot of pasta or make a sandwich. In the living room, there was an old loveseat that Jessica, my Merrill Lynch manager, had given to me. It was beige with a pink-and-green floral pattern, but I kept it covered with a blue sheet to hide the hair from her dog that used to love to sleep on it. There was a small Sony television and VCR combo unit that Jessica had also given to me. It was the smallest I had ever seen, and the loveseat was torn up from wear, but these gifts gave me solace.

Blockbuster Video had a discounted deal at the time: thirty movies in thirty days for thirty dollars. I used to leave work every day, stop at Blockbuster on Poway Road on my way home, take my time picking out one movie, and go home to watch it.

Each movie transferred me to a different world. Watching fictitious lives and struggles on the screen, I felt safer and happier. I used to forget about my life for one or two hours and become immersed in a story of love, family members supporting one other, or an adventure that filled my imagination with possibilities. I remember holding the movie of the day once I picked it up from the shelf at Blockbuster and feeling an immediate sense of anticipation to get home, lock the door, close the two blinds, throw my work clothes on the bed, and get into my PJs.

I used to fill my blue mug with Honey Smacks cereal and milk, get a plastic spoon from the squeaky kitchen drawer that was difficult to open, and take this cold dinner into the living room. I would place the mug next to the loveseat on the carpet and then put the video in the VCR. When the movie started, I would pick up my mug and eat my cereal while I was immersed in the events on-screen. This was my safe, peaceful space, and I did not want to be anywhere else or talk to anyone. Sometimes, I watched the same movie two or three times in one night. But most of the time, I fell asleep on the loveseat and woke up in the middle of the night, not knowing how long I had been sleeping. Then I turned the television off and went to my mattress to sleep a few more hours before waking and repeating the day.

At nineteen, I'd imagined that I was Juliet and Malek was Romeo and that, like them, we'd fallen in love at first sight. And like them, our families were our obstacle, but unlike Romeo and Juliet, who both ended up dead, we would live out a happy ending. Now I was watching fictional romances on my screen because they made me feel better. At the same time, my romantic ideal—the *Romeo and Juliet* version of love—had been shaken; my concepts of love, marriage, and community were shaken, and I had to question these happy endings.

Once when I was at work, a client mentioned she was graduating soon from the University of San Diego. She was working on her master's. When she told me, my heart skipped the way it had skipped when I'd first met Malek. USD was the Catholic university I'd fallen in love with the day Malek and I had attended a wedding there. Somewhere inside me, there was still the seed I'd buried when Malek told me he didn't want me to pursue my master's degree. Watching my movies, I was too depressed to think about it clearly at the time, but maybe I would discover a truer, more successful relationship with my education.

My favorite movie was *You've Got Mail*. Watching Tom Hanks and Meg Ryan play star-crossed, Internet-romance lovers, discover that they are real-life business rivals, and then watching them work past their conflict gave me a sense of hope for the future. I loved that they were equally matched, in heart and head. This became my ideal. I wanted a match in heart and head. I ended up buying my own copy, and if the movie of the day turned out to be dull or too depressing, I would immediately replace it with *You've Got Mail*.

Almost every night while the movie played, I heard my neighbors on the first floor fighting. They were a married couple, and they had a child who was three or four years old. The fights would get so loud and violent that sometimes, by the end of the night, I would see red and blue lights flashing against my blinds.

There was the life I was living, and there was the life I imagined living. In the life I was living, sometime in June, the world started falling apart.

One day around noon, I was in my office and saw that I had a voicemail on my cell phone. When I played the message, I heard Malek's brother. In the past, our discussions had always been minimal and formal. I think this was the first time he had ever called my cell phone. He was yelling, "I am not going to allow you to hurt my brother. You better watch yourself, because I will find a way to hurt you." Then his voice sounded even angrier as he said, "You are a thief! You stole from my parents. We are missing a Christmas wreath. You better bring it back, or I will notify the police."

The claim was absurd and petty, and of course I had not taken a wreath. But this accusation over a small item, which was delivered with so much rage, made his threat and his anger more terrifying and more real. I held the cell phone in my right hand as I listened to the voicemail and stared at the pile of paperwork in

front of me on the desk. The work needed to be completed before the stock market closed on the East Coast, in less than an
hour. One-third of the screen was blinking with green and red as
the stock prices went up and down, and my brain and body were
completely frozen. I put down my phone and stared at the small
webcast of MSNBC on the top right-hand corner of my screen;
a reporter was speaking, but I had the volume turned off. The
blinking stock tickers and the reporter talking on mute were the
only things moving in front of me. I sat at my desk staring for at
least twenty minutes, with both of my hands glued on my cheeks
as if I were trying to keep my head in place.

I could not work, and I could not process this voicemail. I was
stunned that anyone would leave such a nasty, threatening voicemail. I did not know who to call for help in case Malek's brother
actually tried to hurt me. I did not have close family or close
friends in San Diego. I did not think that Auntie Mariam would
be able to help, and I did not want to continue to overload her
with my troubles. The one friend I had was someone with whom
I'd graduated from San Diego State about two years before I left
Malek, but I was not in touch with her. I felt terrified, not just because of the voicemail message but also for the security of my job.
I needed this job to survive, but I was too overwhelmed to get my
work done, and I knew that my performance had been negatively
impacted since March.

As I sat at my desk, unable to function, Jessica walked by my
cubicle. She immediately realized that I did not look okay.

"Dima, what's going on? What's happening?" she asked.

I did not feel comfortable sharing with her because she was my
manager. I was concerned that my job could be endangered if she
knew my personal life might be affecting my job performance,
but Jessica ended up becoming an ally and protector. She stood
waiting for me to respond, and finally, I said, "I have a personal
situation that I am dealing with."

She sat at the chair next to my cubicle and looked at me, waiting for me to talk. She must have been able to see how paralyzed I looked, especially since I was crying uncontrollably, letting my tears drop without a thought.

"I just received a voicemail from my brother-in-law," I said, finally. "He is threatening to hurt me, and I do not know what to do if he actually tries." I picked up my phone and played the voicemail for her. I watched her eyes get wide. This was the first time I saw my own terror over my life reflected on someone else's face, which made me even more terrified. Yet it also helped me feel strangely relieved, because I realized I was not inventing my fears.

She said, "You need to go to the police right after work and share this voicemail with them. I'll drive behind you to make sure no one is following you. I want you to stay at my house tonight. I want to make sure that you're safe."

That night, she prepared a home-cooked meal for me, gave me a manicure, and dyed my hair. When it was dry, she put a tiara on my head. I was experiencing the worst day in my life, and she created a safe environment for me and one that distracted me from reality. More than this, she treated me like I was deserving and like I mattered.

Two days later, back at my apartment, on a Saturday at 7:00 a.m., I woke up to the sound of the phone ringing. I jumped out of bed and picked it up from the floor. Sometimes a ringing phone is a lifeline. Sometimes it stops my breath.

I held the receiver to my ear and said, "Hello?" Immediately, I heard my father's voice on the other end of the line.

"Dima," he said. I was relieved to hear his voice.

I had been planning to call him that day after I woke up. I planned to tell him about the message Malek's brother had left, my visit to the police station, and that the police had called Malek's brother to tell him to leave me alone or I would file a restraining order. However, as my father continued speaking, I realized he sounded angry.

"Your aunties, *my* four sisters, asked me today about your situation with Malek. They told me that they are hearing a lot of gossip about you leaving him."

I got up and walked into the living room. I began opening the blinds to let the sunlight in as I listened. My heart beat faster, and I could feel panic rising into my neck and face. I stared at the pool.

Then he made the most shocking statement: "Our entire community is talking about you, Dima. They're saying you disobeyed your husband and destroyed your marriage. Your action has put my face in the ground. Malek was not man enough to call me and ask me to have you back, but I can no longer allow this to happen. As of today," he told me, "you have two options: Either to go back to your husband—which will end this community gossip—and just deal with your situation; you will not be the first woman to be unhappy in her marriage. Or, option two: I will never want to hear your voice, ever again. I will consider you dead."

I sensed the rage in his tone; it was a sound that brought me back to my childhood. I looked out of the window at the perfect blue pool water reflecting the clear sky on that beautiful San Diego morning, and I felt completely disoriented. I could not understand what was happening. My life was the kind of drama I would have turned off to replace with a simple, happy romance; everything felt unreal.

Then my father said, in a quiet and firm tone, "Which one will you choose?"

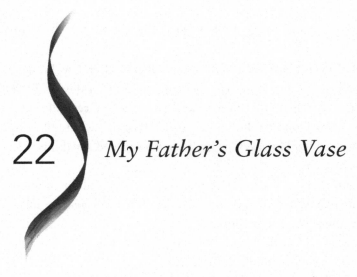

22 $\rangle$ *My Father's Glass Vase*

My father has his own glass vase to maintain and protect. He is a fish inside it, swimming around and around, always looking out from the inside. He thinks that the world ends with the clear and perfect glass edge that blends with the color of the air outside it. The edge of the bowl is the end of the universe in his small world, yet he doesn't realize that this edge is a confining boundary that limits his world.

He checks the glass from top to bottom every time he goes around, believing that it is his responsibility to protect it, making sure that it has no crack, because any crack means that his world would end. A crack would result in water leaking out drop by drop with shame from his world; it would be beyond his control to stop it once the vase is cracked. If the water level falls to the bottom, it cuts off his oxygen; it suffocates him. The slow death makes him want to take immediate revenge. Maybe a harsh action will glue the crack and make his vase appear clear again.

He was dropped in the vase the moment his cord was cut to separate him from his mother's womb. He was told to protect the pure perfect glass vase, not only for his sake but also for the sake of his father, grandfather, great-grandfather, and every single man who shares his family name. He was told to do anything in his power, even if it causes pain and horror to others.

My father had supported my decision to leave Malek. His support had given me a sense of safety and protection; it had given me the energy and assurance to continue surviving the worst period in my life. It had even increased my admiration for him; I had felt close to him for the first time. I had never had a close relationship with my father before, especially after Malek and I got engaged. During our engagement, my main goal had been to do whatever I could to keep my father emotionally stable so he would not destroy my relationship with Malek or decide to end our engagement in the blink of an eye.

After his call that morning, my world collapsed in slow motion. One sentence replayed in my head: "Malek was not man enough to call me and ask me to have you back." I realized for the first time that my father had his own agenda. My father and Malek had been in an invisible battle since the day of my engagement; they were like two fierce bulls unleashed in an arena, their nostrils flaring, their hooves kicking back dirt, and their horns clashing, each man trying to force the other into submission.

The same motivation moved my father to pretend to support me in leaving Malek. My father imagined that my departure from my marriage would be temporary, that it was a temper tantrum. He also imagined that my act would force Malek to go to him and beg for his help convincing me to go back to my marriage. My father's support had not been about my safety, happiness, respect, or independence. His version of support was about maintaining control over me and gaining control over Malek; he wanted me to go back to Malek so that Malek would be indebted to him.

I remembered Uncle Anton's words after I first left Malek: "Don't look back. Don't think of going back to Malek. Move forward with your life; just move on."

But I could not follow this advice anymore. I didn't think I could live with a shattered vase, with being disowned, or with shame reflecting off me and, as a result, onto my parents.

"Baba," I told my father as I stood staring blankly out of my window, "I will fix the situation with Malek. I never want to bring you shame."

"Allah yirda alaiki," he responded, his boiling rage reduced to a simmer from losing his own power gamble—may God bless you.

I hung up the phone and collapsed onto the carpet; my feet did not have the strength to hold me up. I felt worthless, as if I existed for the sole purpose of satisfying confusing, conflicting, and controlling forces.

A pile of used white tissues crumpled and soaked with tears was on the carpet in front of me. I was sitting on the floor in the corner of the living room staring at the two items I had in that room: the worn-out loveseat and the tiny television.

I cleared my tears, but that didn't stop new ones from forming. Then I held the phone and dialed Malek's number while covering my eyes with my free hand, as if this would prevent me from seeing my new, harsh reality.

"Hello, Malek," I said.

Right away, he replied, "How dare you call the police on my brother."

I took a deep breath. "Malek, I am calling to talk to you about getting back together."

He paused and then answered, "I told you already that any-time you want to come back, I would take you back." He spoke like a cat that had caught a mouse. Then he continued, "There are conditions that I need to make clear to you up front, and you have to agree to each of them in order for me to take you back."

I knew I did not want to go back to Malek, but I stayed on the phone listening to him and crying silently. As he spoke, my tears dropped faster and faster.

"First, once we are back together, you can see your parents once a month, but that's it. I do not want them to influence our marriage. I have no desire to visit them or see them, especially your father."

I was in a strange situation of forcing myself to go back to Malek to satisfy my father's demands and honor. But in return, I was expected to follow a condition of not seeing my father other than once a month to satisfy Malek's demands.

"Second, I do not want you to have any communication with your uncle Anton. I believe that he is the one behind all the mess that we are dealing with now."

His voice was firm, like my father's had been a few minutes be-fore. With each condition, I felt the pressure building in my chest. I wanted to scream at the top of my lungs, but when I opened my mouth, not a single sound came out. I was silent, just like I'd been trained to be.

I felt like I was standing in the middle of a rickety old suspen-sion bridge made of ropes and thin wooden planks, while rapids tumbled wildly below me. It was as if my father was standing on safe ground at one end of the bridge, holding a knife and threat-ening to cut the ropes if I didn't obey him, and Malek was on steady ground at the other end, holding his own knife and threatening to cut the ropes if I didn't obey *him*. I felt that I could try to stand perfectly still in the center, waiting for the bridge to collapse on its own or waiting for one of them to cut the ropes. No matter what, I would fall into the rapids. No matter what, my life was over.

"Third," I heard Malek continue, "I do not want you to complain about my family, and especially my mother. If you disagree with her, just keep it to yourself."

As he spoke, I felt a horrible sense of loneliness. I knew I was not safe with Malek or my father.

"It is going to be difficult," I heard Malek say, "for my parents to accept you again; they no longer want you to be part of our family. So fourth, you will need to put in an effort to make them want you back in our family. And fifth, I do not want you to work anymore. I will support us financially. Once you get back to Jordan, I want you to get pregnant and then take care of me, our children, and the house."

Listening to these conditions, my mind seemed disconnected from my body. I heard Malek's words, as my father's words also replayed in my head, but my mind was somewhere else. I saw myself running away from my father. I imagined the sound of my bare feet pounding against the wooden planks as I ran—not toward Malek but past him—to safety, because I felt violated by both men.

Yet I knew that it wasn't just the women who had glass vases to protect. My father had his own vase to protect; Malek had his own vase to protect. The men, in order to protect their own conditioned image of masculinity, needed to control the women, but I was done being controlled by others. By moving back to Jordan and returning to my marriage, I knew my life would become more miserable and controlled than I had ever experienced before.

At last—their voices, the sound of the planks on the bridge, my heart beating fast—everything quieted. All I could hear was the voice inside my heart repeating, *I can't go back to this. I can't go back to this. I can't go back to this.*

After he finally finished listing the conditions of my return, I responded, "Malek, I do not want that life." That was the last sentence I ever spoke directly to Malek. That was our last phone call.

I often used to sleep to escape reality. That afternoon, I went to my bed in the middle of the day and slept hard. Hours later, I woke up remembering the dream I'd been having. In it, I was alone on a small and simple wooden raft. I was surrounded by water, with no land in sight. As I was paddling, I sensed that someone was behind me. I turned around to look, and I found my sister, Ruba, who was seventeen at the time, sleeping behind me on the raft. She was lying perfectly still. Her face looked almost peaceful, but we were on the raft for the same reason. I was trying to paddle both of us to safety.

23 Celebrations

That Fourth of July, Auntie Mariam invited me to a barbecue at Lake Poway. She had supported my decision from the beginning to the end, even when my father turned against me, and she insisted that I come to the event.

"Dima, you need a change of scenery," she told me.

"Auntie Mariam, I need to study for the GMAT," I responded. I am signed up to take it in a month. I need to prepare."

This was true. I was still spending a lot of time losing myself in movies, but I'd also transferred some of my depression into studying. I would come home, change into pajamas, pour a bowl of cereal, and settle into my bed with two pillows propped up behind my back. I kept my pen, highlighter, and calculator nearby and opened my notebook and a thick study guide. I would work my way through practice tests and explanations until I fell asleep, burrowed under the calming aqua-blue sheets.

However, studying for the GMAT was not the real reason I didn't want to go to the barbecue. "Auntie Mariam, I am not in a mental place to celebrate anything," I admitted. "I don't think I can be around people who will be curious about why I left Malek, especially since many of them know Malek and his family."

"Dima," she said, "you need to take a break. It will be good for you." So, reluctantly, I agreed.

There must have been thirty people gathered in her group. As I expected, many women, one by one, sat on the plastic white chair next to me and began, "I heard about Malek and you. What happened?"

Each time, I answered as quickly as I could, trying to shift the conversation to the good food and the cute children playing and laughing around us. As I navigated these conversations, I wished I could be alone in my apartment, sitting in the dark and under the covers of my bed. Finally, the sun went down and the fireworks started.

I found unexpected pleasure in seeing the dark sky light up with explosions of color that faded into streaks of smoke before more bursts of color painted the blackness. I hadn't enjoyed anything in months, but for those few minutes, my mind was distracted from my own circumstances. Watching the fireworks, I felt a tiny spark of joy before I said my good-byes. Along with all of the other people who'd come to celebrate, I walked to my car to head home.

I was sitting in the parking lot in bumper-to-bumper traffic around 9:30 p.m. when my cell phone rang. As I watched the traffic, I pulled my ringing phone out of my purse. My mother was calling from Jordan, where it must have been after 7:30 a.m. The image of fireworks was still in my head when I answered.

"Hi, Mama," I answered.

"Hi," she replied in a voice so weak that she sounded farther away than she already was. I realized that something was wrong.

"What is going on?" I asked.

"Listen, Dima," she said, as if she hardly had the energy to get the words out. "The situation has been terrible here. I came into the office early so I could call you in private." She paused and took a breath. I listened carefully. Though she was composed, I was sure that she was crying. "Your father is not able to handle the fact that you are getting a divorce. It is bringing him shame that he cannot process, and his temper is getting worse each day."

The fireworks in my head faded. My life was already smashed into pieces, but now, for the first time, I was beginning to feel the pain from those shards. It seemed that they had finally broken through the skin.

"Your father is getting drunk every night. He is out of control." She continued, "I have had to call your uncles every night for the last two weeks to come over and help calm him down."

My mind flashed to six years earlier. The year of my engagement, my father spent nearly every Friday, his first weekend day off from work, alone, and brooding as the hours passed. By the late afternoon, already agitated, he started drinking. As he drank, he got angrier and angrier thinking about the ways he felt he had been insulted by Malek or his parents. In this drunken state, he would start petty arguments with my mom or me and my siblings until his temper escalated and he was suddenly screaming, breaking glass, and destroying anything he could get his hands on. Once he was in a state of rage, we used to call Uncle Zaid up from his home on the second floor to help calm my father down. If Uncle Zaid wasn't available, or if we thought my father's own brother, Uncle Jaffar, who lived twenty minutes away, would have better results, we called him instead.

"We have a 'celebration' going on," we used to tell them, and they understood immediately that this was code for my father's rages. They talked to my father until they began to calm him down, assuring him that he was right and that everyone would follow his desires going forward.

"It is worse this time than any other," my mother said, as if she knew I was remembering the past. "He's not just getting drunk and breaking glass cups." She paused and took another breath.

"What do you mean?" I asked.

"Every night, after he gets drunk, he beats me. Sometimes in front of Ruba. He says, 'How dare you put my face in the ground? You and your daughter brought me shame. I will teach you a lesson that you will never forget. I will make you a topic of discussion that other women will learn from.'" She lowered her voice and said, full of her own shame, "It's the middle of summer, and I'm wearing high necks with scarves and long-sleeved shirts and long skirts when I come to work. I have bruises all over my body, and I don't want my coworkers to see them."

I gasped when I heard this, but I could not speak. I was staring at children twirling the last of their sparklers and walking with their parents to their cars. In the headlights, I could see the kids' faces filled with the hope of boundless possibilities and happy exhaustion after a fun day celebrating the country's independence.

"He has decided that we all deserve to die. Me. You. Ruba. He says he is going to murder me and your sister, then fly to America to murder you, and finally, he will kill himself."

I sat quietly trying to take in these words. I saw my life appear in front of my eyes like a giant mirror that had no frame to hold it in place. Without support, it fell on the floor. In the split second it took to hit the ground, it shattered. The shards flew in all directions and covered the ground; their edges were sharp and unavoidable. This felt like the end of the world.

Listening to my mother, I had a deep sense of regret for my decision; it was causing my entire family turmoil and misery. I thought of what my father used to say after the final scene in Bedouin movies, the moment after the woman is killed for dishonoring her family. Satisfied with the ending, he used to proclaim, "Blood erases shame and brings lost honor back to the family."

Suddenly, it occurred to me that I was one of the women I had heard Tata and her friends gossiping about over coffee; I was the shameful woman in the last scene of a Bedouin movie.

Every time my mother spoke, she delivered another heart-break. "He's sleeping with a meat cleaver under the bed," she told me. "Ruba wakes up every morning thanking God that she is still alive and that he did not get emotional during the night and stab her to death in her sleep."

When I had first uttered a word about my unhappiness to my mother in November, she had warned me about the consequences, and Tata had been explaining the consequences of breaking my vase since I was five years old. At that moment, envisioning Ruba sleeping with her eyes open in the night and my mother's bruised body, I knew I was experiencing the consequences of shattering my vase.

I could not breathe anymore, and my head became too heavy to hold up. I was still sitting in traffic with the cars barely moving out of the driveway and onto the street. I was holding the steering wheel with my left hand and the cell phone with my right. I put my head on the steering wheel and moved my left hand to cover my eyes, trying to block the image my mother was describing.

I started questioning my decision again. How stupid of me, I thought. What was I thinking? Maybe dealing with Malek, his mother, and his family could have been easy. Maybe I should have just stayed quiet and obedient.

"There is more," my mother said.

I did not think I could handle any more, but I didn't think she could say anything worse than what she had already shared.

"Even worse than the drinking and the beatings and the knife," my mother said, "he has ordered a gun."

My hearing, sight, and all of my senses stopped working. I felt like I had been placed in a void, and I wanted to disappear into it.

"I can't take this anymore," my mother said, and she burst out crying. We were thousands of miles apart, but we were both cry-ing together. We both knew our futures could be determined by a man who could, without thinking, pull a trigger to end our lives for the sake of preserving his honor.

Cars started moving, but I did not have the energy to drive. I pulled over and parked on the side of the road. Sitting in the dark, I watched as the other cars drove home, the passengers happy after a celebration.

24   *Half Dead*

The first time my mother tried to leave her marriage, I was less than two years old. My mother went to Tata and begged for help.

"Take your baby and go back to your husband," Tata told her. "I will not permit my daughter to get divorced. Don't you know that no family will approve of their daughter marrying any of your brothers if you are divorced?"

My mother carried me on her hip and walked back home to her husband.

Twenty-five years later, my mother went to visit her eldest brother, my uncle Qader, to ask for help a second time in her life. This time, instead of having her two-year-old with her, she went with my seventeen-year-old sister, Ruba.

My mother did not tell me what she was wearing that day, but every time I think about it, I imagine her in a long black dress with long sleeves and plain black shoes with low heels. There is no jewelry on her body, just black fabric covering red skin and blue and green bruises.

These are the things I know with certainty about that day: At 4:00 a.m. San Diego time and 2:00 p.m. Amman time, I called my mother's office. When she answered the phone, she sounded half dead.

"How did it go?" I asked.

"Not good," my mother responded. She stopped and said, "Wait. I am going to close my office door." When she returned to the phone, she started sobbing while trying to talk about the details of the visit. "I dropped Ruba off at home and returned to work after our visit," my mother said. "It was a mistake to share what we are experiencing with your uncle Qader. I should have known better. He listened to what we had to say, all of it, and he looked at the bruises. But he was only worried about his reputation. He kept saying that if we left, this situation would impact him."

I was sitting on my bed in the dark. Slivers of light from a bulb outside my window were streaming into the room through cracks in the blinds, making striped lines across my wall.

"He told me there are only two solutions," my mother said: "'Either go home and figure out a way to calm the situation with your husband and get back to your normal life, or tell Dima to meet with Malek, find a middle ground, and go back to him.'" My mother paused, and the two of us breathed silently together over the phone. I said nothing.

"He told me, 'If you and Ruba dare to plan to leave Jordan, I will personally call your husband and tell him of your plans.'"

Again, I said nothing. I was afraid my mother would give me the same ultimatum my father had given to me.

To my shock, she said, "Dima, we have to find a way to leave Jordan. Ruba and I can no longer stay." A mix of relief and terror washed through my body at once.

A day later, I was at work in front of my computer and checking e-mail when I saw a new e-mail from Ruba. I opened it and read the words: "Dima, please help us." Bolts of anger and sadness shot through my chest. I knew we needed to make a plan right away, but I did not have the resources to get them out.

Once Malek no longer had hope that I would go back, he had

his attorney reach out to mine. He was worried that I would ask for half of his wealth. This was something he had always been concerned about; it was part of the reason he never bought a house for us when we moved to the States. He used to say, "In America, the wife always ends up with the house and half of the wealth." He was fixated on this cultural difference; the rights women had in the States clashed with his belief system.

His attorney drafted an agreement. It stated that I would release my rights to any properties, investments, or assets he owned. In return, he would release the right to request alimony.

Our last year of marriage, while he was in Jordan, he was not earning income in the States. So, technically, he could claim that I had supported him over the last year with my salary of thirty thousand dollars, which in reality could barely support the two of us. I did not want his money. I just wanted my sanity, to be able to move on and leave the past behind. I agreed to his terms. However, leaving the past behind wasn't as simple as that.

It was a matter of chance that both Ruba and my mother had their green cards. When Uncle Anton had immigrated to the United States in the 1970s and then became a citizen, he submitted green card applications for our entire family. We all received them in 1995, a year before I got married. Now we took advantage of this blessing.

Auntie Nadia agreed to help us with a plan that would not cause my father and Uncle Qader any suspicions. She called my father and asked for his permission to have Ruba visit her in Toronto for two weeks in August before the school year started; Ruba was set to attend her first year of university, so this would be a high school graduation gift. Auntie Nadia offered to pay for

Ruba's airfare and cover all of her expenses. She made this generous offer so my father could not use money as an excuse to decline.

In the meantime, my mother invented a story that she was required to go on a two-day business trip to Malta. My father had never allowed her to travel for business in the past, not even within Jordan, but surprisingly, he agreed. When he gave his consent, she used some of her own savings to book a one-way flight from Amman to Los Angeles.

Ruba was terrified by our father's death threats, his drunken rages, and seeing him beat our mother. However, she was also not happy about the plan to flee to Canada and then move to America. In many ways, she had a comfortable life. She loved her friends. She enjoyed being the only child in our parents' home after Waseem moved to New Mexico in 1995 and I moved to San Diego in 1996. She loved the little colorful stuffed animals with hearts that she had acquired over the years from friends and family. These decorated her room and created a comfortable safe space for her. Even with my father's abuse, the idea of leaving every last belonging and relationship behind was overwhelming and difficult to accept.

My mother and I reminded her repeatedly not to share the plan with anyone, not even her closest friends. A few days before the flight, it came out that she had shared everything with her best friend, Lana. She had promised not to tell anyone, but now we were more anxious than ever. We couldn't be certain that Ruba's friend would not share the plan with others and ruin the chances of escaping, which could have resulted in deadly consequences.

In the days leading up to August 10, my mother tried to act normal so my father would not become suspicious. She did whatever he asked of her. Before the day she departed, he took her to the bank and requested that she release all the funds from their joint account into his name alone. She did it without hesitation.

She knew that what she was planning would help her gain her freedom and would save Ruba. These two acts were bigger than my father's control and bigger than the entire community's judgment and the expectations that had suffocated her all her life. She prayed to the Virgin Mary, all day long, every minute, for the escape to go smoothly.

To this day, it seems like a miracle that my father approved both trips. Maybe he felt guilty for his irrational behavior; maybe it was divine intervention. What matters is that he approved. My mother coordinated both trips to depart from Amman's Queen Alia International Airport on the same connecting flight through Amsterdam. The flight was scheduled to leave at 8:00 p.m. on August 10, 2001. My father drove them both to the airport. He had a Jordanian diplomat passport, called the Red Passport, and with it, he walked them through security to their flight gate, unknowingly ushering them to their new life.

My mother continued to pray, as if Mother Mary were dedicated only to her that day. My father was erratic, so she was worried that he would change his mind at the last minute and tell one or both of them she could not travel. She would never have left without Ruba. My mother kept watching his body language; she had learned it well over the years. She was looking for any alarming clue. But mainly, she was worried that he would sense what had been planned. If he began to suspect anything, she knew it would be the end of her life.

Finally, he said good-bye to both of them and left, not realizing that this was the last time he would ever see them. At seventeen, just two months after Ruba had completed the *Tawjihi*, she had no other choice but to walk away from the only life she knew; my mother, at forty-nine, faced the same single choice.

As my mom and sister were in the air flying out west on two separate planes, I was in a quiet room taking the GMAT and trying hard to stay focused. In the midst of turmoil, preparing for my mother and sister's escape, I found comfort in putting my mind to something safe.

I got my results immediately after the exam. I didn't do well. I went home that afternoon feeling disappointed but not surprised and knowing that it was going to be my last night alone in the apartment.

In Amsterdam, my sister boarded a plane to Toronto. Two hours later, my mother flew to Los Angeles. It was the first time she had ever been separated from Ruba.

When my mother exited the customs and immigration area at the Los Angeles airport's international terminal, she was surrounded by passengers who seemed impatient after a long flight. They hurried past her, rolling carts filled with many large and heavy bags containing belongings, gifts, and souvenirs from other countries. When I saw my mother, she was standing still, holding her purse and one small carry-on that contained enough clothes to last her for two days. She had nothing else.

Stepping onto American soil, across the world from the place she had called home her entire life, meant leaving everything familiar behind. She didn't lose only material items like her home, her car, the savings she had built up from her job, and the gold she had grown up believing symbolized her worth as a woman. She also left behind sentimental gifts from Tata, treasured photographs from her childhood and from her children's childhoods, and she became disconnected from her family and friends for the first time in her life. Her worst heartache was that her two brothers in Jordan had not supported her when she needed them.

I entered the airport and walked toward her. Just a few months earlier, I had picked her up at the same terminal. Then, she still had hope that I would return to Malek. Now, she was drained of that hope for me, and she was drained of hope for herself. She looked like she had aged twenty years since the last time I saw her. Her face looked pale, sad, and terrified; it looked as if she were under a dark cloud, standing in the silent, still center of a cyclone.

When I got to her, she did not say anything. Neither did I. We embraced each other and stood there crying—for a minute, or ten, or more, I do not remember. I knew she held only a single grain of hope—the very basic desire to stay alive. We were both thankful to God that she had made it to the United States without my father realizing that her trip was really an escape plan.

When we let go of each other, the first words out of her mouth were, "We need to call Nadia and make sure Ruba made it to Toronto." Concern spilled out in her voice.

In the middle of the Los Angeles airport, I pulled an international calling card from my wallet and dialed its number and code before calling Auntie Nadia. Then I put the phone on speaker. My mother and I were frozen as we waited for the news. The first thing Auntie Nadia said was, "She is here. Ruba is here with me. She landed safely." My mother and I maintained eye contact as we listened to Auntie Nadia's relieved voice. We could breathe again.

We walked out to my car, the Volkswagen I'd purchased after I started working at Merrill Lynch. My small act of joyful insistence to put the car in my name alone was the only reason I still had transportation.

I felt crushed every time I saw my mother from the corner of my eye. She looked broken, both physically and emotionally. She was mostly quiet for the entire two-hour drive from the airport to my apartment in San Diego.

She stared at the cars in front of us, and the only movement she made was to blink once in a while. She looked as if the fluids in her body had evaporated and she had physically shrunk from the loss she was feeling.

"You're safe, Mama," I whispered. "We did it." I wanted to cry as I drove, but I held it in as long as I could.

All she could say in return was, "I don't want to be a burden, Dima. I don't want to be a burden."

Tears streamed down my face one by one, hidden behind my sunglasses.

A week later, on August 18, 2001, Ruba left Canada and arrived in San Diego. This was the final step in our plan. This was the day the three of us started our new lives together. After we picked up Ruba from the airport, we went to a movie theater and watched *Legally Blonde*. We wanted to forget, for a few hours, the horrible experience we were living through. I remember laughing together. Yet this was also the day that all communication with my father stopped. The phone line to Jordan went silent, dead. This was self-preservation, self-protection, and we knew it was not going to be easy.

In the same year, in two different countries, both my mother and I divorced our husbands. My parents' marriage lasted twenty-seven years, and mine lasted five.

25 Surviving

At twenty-five, newly divorced, and still relatively new to the United States, I held in my hands the responsibility for the well-being of my mother and my sister. This hit me for the first time on that drive from the airport to San Diego. Before that day, I had believed that by shattering my vase, I would live with the consequences of my one shattered vase, as Tata warned me I would. But with my mother's arrival, I suddenly understood the magnitude of that shatter. Its vibration shook the ground and radiated to my mother and Ruba, shattering their vases as well. Over the next three years, I put aside my heartbreak and guilt and concentrated on their well-being.

Auntie Mariam had warned us of the short, simple threat my father had begun making after my mother and Ruba escaped. Along with countless other lies he had invented about us to anyone who would listen, he repeatedly warned: "If any of them dares to return to Jordan, I will make them minced meat."

He promised to kill the three of us to save face. Though he did not speak those words directly to me, I could easily hear the tone of his voice, and I could see his eyes filled with anger and disgrace.

We had a safety ritual for every time we entered our apartment. Together, we walked up the narrow, open-air stairwell that led to a landing area that doubled as a small balcony. It was just big enough to place a couple of chairs and a potted plant outside our front door. I unlocked the door and flung it wide open. Then I stood guard outside on the balcony, held my pepper spray, and peeked inside while also scanning the parking lot for unfamiliar cars and signs of danger. My mother and Ruba quietly entered, each armed with her own pepper spray. They moved through the apartment, checking behind the doors of the bedroom, dressing room, and bathroom and turning on lights. In the bedroom, they looked behind and underneath the bed.

Over the three years that we lived together, we repeated our safety ritual many times. Every time, standing at the door, it was as if I were watching the same old movie but noticing something new with each viewing. There was a lot to witness—I saw what was happening in the actual moment, and I saw what was happening over time.

The first year was the hardest. That year, as I watched my mother flipping on switches and turning darkened rooms to brightly lit, I could see her devastation unfold. In an instant, she lost everything that took a lifetime to build. Her physical body was present, but her grief and loss hollowed her from the inside out. It was hard to watch. I remember her moving through our sparse apartment each day; every step was a challenge as she struggled to adapt to a new, strange life in a new country. As months passed, I saw her body become paler and thinner. She was weighted down by the pain caused by her two brothers in Jordan who had not supported her at the lowest moment in her life.

She heard about the lies my father was telling our community in Amman; she knew they'd ruined her reputation and honor. That weight was depleting her spirit and body, making it seem as if she were slowly disappearing.

Getting accustomed to living in the United States and gaining a sense of independence were not easy. She had learned English in Jordan, but she was not fluent. Now, she was abruptly immersed in an English-speaking country. She realized that what she knew in her head did not match what she could do in practice.

While I was growing up, many women did not learn to drive a car. My mother didn't learn to drive until a few years before she left Amman, and it had been a small source of freedom. Though she could operate a vehicle and had learned the rules of the road, her insecurity about speaking and writing English held her back. She failed the written portion of the driver's test four times before she finally passed the California driving exam.

With every failure, she felt lower, not just because she couldn't legally drive but also because she was repeatedly reminded of the skills she didn't possess to survive in this country. If she couldn't drive, if she couldn't easily speak or quickly read and write English, she couldn't get a job; she couldn't earn a living; she couldn't be self-sufficient. What hurt her more was that if she needed to, she couldn't even help her own children.

About two months after my mom and sister arrived in San Diego, I started getting a bad pain in the right side of my lower back. I kept ignoring it, hoping that it would just go away on its own. After about a week, on a Saturday afternoon, the pain got so bad that I could no longer stand up and I started throwing up.

Without a license to drive, or the confidence to speak English well, Ruba and my mother were paralyzed. They could not drive to take me to the doctor. My mother did not even know how to get to the ER. She would not know what to say to the doctor, even if she'd managed to get me to the hospital. She and Ruba had to watch me suffer on the floor, knowing there was nothing they could do to help.

We called 911, and we called one of my coworkers from Merrill Lynch who lived close by so she could support my mom and Ruba. But my coworker arrived after the EMS. The technicians would not let my mom and sister get into the ambulance with me. Both of them were crying as they watched the EMS technicians carry me down the stairs of our apartment, into the ambulance, and then drive away.

"That was the absolute lowest moment in my life," my mom told me when she finally saw me in the hospital, "to see you taken away in front of my eyes. I did not know where they were taking you, and I could not even follow them in a car. I have never felt so helpless." It turned out that I had a small, treatable kidney stone, and I was released late that night. But this experience was another indication of how fragile we were.

I also struggled watching Ruba's transition to the States. My eighteen-year-old sister's life had been interrupted before it ever began. I observed her becoming more and more depressed. Just as my mother seemed to be vanishing, Ruba seemed to be carrying the weight of two separate worlds with her each day. Many mornings, when I'd go into the kitchen to make my lunch for the day, I found her there eating ice cream from the carton for breakfast. She'd be staring straight ahead, moving the spoon from the carton to her mouth in robotic motions.

I had happily moved to the United States after I got married. Our mom had also made her own decision to come to the United

States when my father's abuse became increasingly dangerous. But Ruba, who saw what was happening and was also frightened, didn't have the same individual choice about moving that we had. Even though she understood that the situation was bad, on some level, this move must have felt forced on her. She was still a teenager, and she must have felt she'd lost all of her belongings and friends, her entire life, without any say in the matter.

Phone calls were still expensive, so the only way she could connect with friends was through e-mail. But every time Ruba received messages from her friends, she became more depressed. That first year, she gained forty pounds; her depression was on display.

There is one happy memory I have from that first year. The day my mother passed her driving exam, the three of us crowded into our kitchen and popped open a bottle of sparkling wine. I can still see us huddled in the kitchen laughing and cheering. I can still hear my mother raising her glass up triumphantly and saying, "Thank you, Virgin Mary." She took a big sip and told us, "I prayed to the Virgin Mary the entire time I took the test. I promised an offering to someone in need if I just passed the test!"

The next day, the three of us piled into the car. My mother took the driver's seat. While we were stopped at a red light, she rolled her window down and handed some cash to a homeless woman who was with a child. She was one step closer to real independence, even if there were hundreds more to go.

During the week, she would wake up early and drive me to work every day so she could keep the car to pick up groceries or to give Ruba rides. She kept my cell phone with her while I was in the office. Everyday around 4:00 p.m., she would call my office number to let me know that she had arrived and was waiting for me in the car. The drive to and from my office became our time to reflect and talk about various things that were happening in our lives. We would talk about our monthly bills, calculating whether we would have enough to pay everything on time. We would discuss new threats from my father, my mother's health, and Ruba's well-being.

But victories were too often interrupted by challenges. My father began writing letters to the US Immigration Department, hoping to cause conflict that would have my mother sent back to Jordan. When I told Uncle Anton about this over a phone call, he suggested that we go to see an attorney. Each month, Uncle Anton and his wife sent us a letter with a check for five hundred dollars to help us out with our expenses. That month, he sent extra money along to pay for the attorney. My mother and I found a reputable attorney in La Jolla, about twenty minutes from our home. When we explained the situation, the attorney said he could help us.

That evening, we used a restaurant gift card I'd received at work. We ordered champagne and a raspberry cheesecake and cheered for the simple concept that there was hope to resolve the situation. We stopped to take in the positive moments when we could, but they were always set against a threatening backdrop.

We were not just living with the fear of death threats; we were fearful for our basic survival. Worrying about whether we would have enough money to pay the rent and buy groceries became as terrifying as the fear of my father appearing at our door. I realized our fear was not going to go away, and I had to learn to protect my mother and sister regardless of fear. Flipping lights on in our apartment as we entered wasn't enough protection.

Our basic survival became my incentive to bring *real* light back into our lives. At last, I was able to fully comprehend what Uncle Anton had tried to impress on me many years before, that my education really could be more than a stepping-stone to marriage. Now, I knew it would *have* to be.

Once the three of us started to fall into a routine, I began studying again, taking GMAT preparation courses on the weekends to improve my score. I retook the test in the spring of 2002. As soon as the results arrived, I was delighted that I'd done well. I had all the other paperwork ready to apply to my dream university, the University of San Diego. While I was waiting anxiously for their letter, one Sunday I drove myself to the campus. I found myself walking toward the Immaculata Catholic Church, going into the chamber with the statue of the Virgin Mary, and praying to her for strength and hope. The next day, I received my acceptance letter in the mail. I held it close to my chest, closed my eyes, and breathed deeply with joy. Next, I picked up the phone and called Uncle Anton. Finally, no one could stop me from pursuing a higher education or from aspiring to expand my potential.

It was early summer by then. We were nearing the end of the most tumultuous year in our lives. It felt like we were about to turn a corner.

We saved money to buy a new couch and gave away the old, torn-up loveseat Jessica had given to me after I left Malek. We gave it to the neighbors who lived below us. They carried it out of our apartment door as the furniture store's delivery men were bringing up our new green couch. When they brought it in, they put it in front of the television, and the three of us watched them remove its protective wrapping while we inhaled the new smell. There was still nothing else in the sitting area, no side tables, no frames on the wall, nothing—just the clean, dark green couch that the three of us could all sit on at once and the old, tiny television. But every time I opened the door and saw it, I smiled.

In the late summer of 2002, we moved out of that one-bedroom in Poway and into a two-bedroom apartment in Rancho Bernardo. I finally convinced myself to return to the storage unit. I pulled open the door and took it in. We went to see what we had that we could use in our new apartment. I opened one of the boxes, and it felt like something horrible spewed out into my face. I shut the box as quickly as I could. I still wasn't ready to deal with those memories, but I'd made the first step.

In our new apartment, we had a rolling laundry cart, and on weekends, my mother and I used to wheel it to the communal laundry room together. We sorted the dirty clothes, loaded them into the washing machines, and then into the dryers. Later, we loaded the warm, clean clothes back into the bin and rolled it up to our apartment together to fold or hang. Just as checking the apartment for intruders had been stressful, doing the laundry became a comforting routine.

In the fall, while continuing to work at Merrill Lynch, I started my MBA program. I was gaining the credentials to specialize in business—the field I had been interested in from the very beginning—and discovering that this private university sitting on a hill overlooking the valley, with a Catholic church at the heart of its campus, truly was the right place for me. Walking into our new, though sparsely furnished apartment and walking onto that campus full of possibility, my feet were firmly set in two different realities; I could sense the promise of something good.

The same year I started courses at USD, my mother and I helped Ruba enroll in college. My mother had been practicing her English skills. She initially worked at a deli and then found an administrative job at a logistics company and was earning a small income, so we pooled our money to pay for Ruba's tuition and expenses.

By our third year of living together, we did not check the apartment every single time we entered; this was a relief. We felt compelled to repeat the ritual only if something happened that shook us—such as hearing of a new lie or threat my father had told to a family friend. I could now stand at the door and scan our surroundings with less immediate fear, and when I peeked inside on my mother and Ruba, instead of grief flashing before my eyes, I witnessed evidence of stability and routine.

Though it eventually faded, our ritual had always ended the same way: After my mother and Ruba finished searching the apartment, they would say in relieved voices, "Ma fish hada." There is no one here. Then, after the three of us were inside, we celebrated the fact that we were all there, together and safe. Before we went to sleep, I used to count our bodies out loud: "One, two, three."

If only I had known that life would turn out to be amazing, I would not have cried so many tears. But at that time, I felt helpless. I didn't know not to cry.

26 *Ettalteh Nabteh*

It was around noon on a day in late October 2002, when I was pursuing my MBA, the first time I heard these words come out of Dr. Starling's mouth: "Student SCMA elections are coming up. You should think about running for president, Dima."

My body tensed up faster than I could respond with words. We were walking with a group of about thirty students who were all members of the University of San Diego's Supply Chain Management Association. We had just finished a site tour at the manufacturing facility for Solar Turbines, and we were heading to the parking lot. I had missed many of the other events that were hosted by SCMA, but this time, I'd taken a half day off work to participate. During the tour, I had lit up and asked question after question.

I closed my eyes and shook my head from side to side as I walked with Dr. Starling. It was an impossible idea. It was more than I could even begin to envision. I opened my eyes and looked into Dr. Starling's bright blue eyes. They were radiating with positive energy.

"I can't run. I do not have the time or skills to be the president," I said.

Dr. Starling jerked his head back in surprise and asked, "What do you mean you don't have the skills?" I was surprised by his surprise.

I had a full-time job, and I was taking MBA classes. Dr. Starling was impressed with my passion to learn and the professional image that I projected. Adding a leadership role in the SCMA to my résumé seemed natural to him. Dr. Starling assumed that I was like any other ambitious American student, and in some ways, externally, I was. But he did not realize that there was a side of my life I kept secret. I was taking care of my mother and helping her and Ruba get more accustomed to living in the States. I was dealing with our family ruins, health issues, the death threats, financial insecurity over our basic survival, and my own lingering heartbreak.

I hoped these wounds would one day disappear. I hoped for a new life; I hoped somehow, someday, to be reborn. In the meantime, I worked hard to keep these personal wounds hidden. They were buried in a well-sealed coffin. Even so, instead of disappearing, I could feel them with me all the time, like internal bleeding.

"I have never had any kind of leadership position in my life," I said.

"You can learn the skills," he replied, his positivity still beaming through his eyes. He seemed completely confident in my ability, which stunned and flattered me. "I'll coach you through it."

Deep down, I wanted to be more active in the student organization. I would have loved to become the president and grow as a leader. But I believed I was in a place in my life that restricted me from even having this dream. I felt limited by my daily responsibilities and my internal circumstances. The thought of adding one more responsibility to my plate felt overwhelming; it seemed like the tipping point that would make everything else I was trying to keep down and under control rise to the surface.

I could see what limited me, but I could not see what might help me move past my limitations. So instead of accepting Dr. Starling's challenge as an opportunity, I started recommending other students whom I thought would be a great fit for this role. Afterward, I thought we were finished with this conversation.

I did not have the same confidence in my ability that Dr. Starling did. My low heels tapped the concrete. I walked with a practical, attainable purpose; I needed to return to the office.

In early November, I walked by a coffee shop on campus and saw Dr. Starling having a discussion with five students. They were a mix of MBA and undergraduate students. It was early evening, and the sky was still blue. The coffee shop faced a beautiful, big fountain, and to its right side, there was the magnificent Immaculata Catholic Church that had made me fall in love with USD when I first stepped foot onto the campus.

I pulled up a chair and joined everyone. Dr. Starling was one of my favorite professors. He often spent time with students outside class, helping us with interview skills, résumé building, and internship opportunities. That day, they were discussing the upcoming SCMA election. Dr. Starling turned to me and said, "I still think that you should run for president, Dima. SCMA is growing. You already have many ideas that can be worked on in the upcoming year. You will do great. I am positive."

I took his words as a compliment, and I smiled enthusiastically. I was intrigued by the idea of growing an organization, but I needed to be realistic. To my surprise, I watched the five students nod in agreement with Dr. Starling's idea. I was still sure that I was not the right fit for the role. Yet again, I thought this was the end of the discussion.

In the Middle East we have a saying, "ettalteh nabteh," which is similar to the Western saying, "the third time's the charm." In other words, things work out on the third try; that was the case in this situation. I was with a group of other MBA students and some undergraduates at the student lounge on the first floor of the business school. It had been renovated recently, and everything looked modern and new. We were excited about the two new flat-screen televisions, the high tables and stools, the new smell of the navy-blue carpet, and the contemporary light fixtures hanging above.

It was after a night class, around 7:30 p.m. in the middle of November. It had been raining nonstop all day, and San Diego was finally turning cooler. Dr. Starling was there with his laptop and stacks of papers that he needed to grade. He was meeting with students, reviewing our résumés, and highlighting sections that we needed to update. When it was my turn to sit with him, I had a feeling that he was going to bring up the same topic all over again. And he did.

He glanced at my résumé, marking it with his pen, and then he looked at me. "You know, being the president of the SCMA will boost your career. The title alone will be a great addition to your résumé."

I knew that his statement was accurate. Many of the current SCMA officers, even undergraduate students, were receiving competitive job offers before graduating. In many cases, they were offered salaries twenty thousand dollars higher than what I was earning at Merrill Lynch. I knew I needed to earn more money, but at the same time my lack of confidence, self-worth, trust in my abilities, and all the other external limitations were stopping me from saying two letters out loud: "O" and "K."

I sat in the new chair with the new carpet beneath my feet and thought over his words. I thought to myself, maybe I should consider it after all. I knew that it was not going to be easy. I knew that it was going to challenge every cell in my body and put me in uncomfortable situations that I usually avoided, and I knew that I would need to work harder than I already was working.

As if he knew I was finally considering the idea, Dr. Starling added, "Companies look for titles and skills like this, not just the high GPA."

I looked at Dr. Starling's serious eyes, seeming to dangle a challenge in front of me. "OK, I will do it," I said, smiling at him. "I will run."

His face brightened instantly with a big smile, and he said, "You will do great."

A few weeks later, at the beginning of December, I was standing outside a classroom located on the first floor of the business school. It was the room that the current SCMA officers used to conduct the voting process. Students were walking in and out of the room, dressed casually in their jeans and T-shirts. It was just after 5:00 p.m., and I had driven over straight from work, so I was still dressed in a black skirt suit with a blue button-down shirt. People walked in and out to cast their votes, smiling or waving hello as they passed me.

Would they really elect me? I did not think I knew anything about being an effective leader. I was convinced that other candidates were better qualified than I was. By the end of the voting process, around 7:00 p.m., the current SCMA president opened the door and walked out of the classroom. The officers had finished counting the votes. I was standing with a group of other students who were also waiting for the results. She walked up to me, smiled, and said, "Congratulations."

The following semester, spring of 2003, in my new position as the SCMA president, I practiced a short opening speech for days. I had never presented in front of a big crowd of strangers before, and I had never stood behind a lectern. As the president, it was my responsibility to open the annual career fair that took place in April. Recruiting managers from national companies would be there, and I knew first impressions mattered.

When I got a signal that it was time to open the event, I walked slowly across the stage floor, while my heart was beating faster and faster and my breath became shorter. I took my place behind the wooden lectern on the right side of the stage. Standing there, I could not speak. The hours I had spent preparing and practicing a welcome speech of less than ten sentences appeared to have been a waste.

Recruiters from national and international companies sat on cushioned blue chairs in a big USD auditorium, waiting. Their front-and-center seats had been reserved for them. In their dark business suits, they looked intensely focused and serious. They each held a white and blue folder that had been given to them as they checked in. On the cover was the USD logo, and inside, there were hard copies of all the presenting students' résumés. Some of the guests were already jotting down notes on the résumés.

The students were seated alphabetically in the rows behind the recruiters. Each was to give a one-minute presentation about his or her background and skills. I was not there to introduce myself as a potential employee, as the other students were; yet I was terrified and intimidated. I was afraid to mess up in front of everyone. I was afraid of being judged by more than two hundred people. Recruiting managers, undergraduate and MBA students, and professors were all sitting comfortably and staring up at me. I had hidden my notes inside the lectern, but that was not enough to calm me down.

I took a moment to scan the room and looked at the audience. I looked at the recruiters first. Then I shifted my attention to the students. I was used to seeing them in colorful beach flip-flops and crumpled T-shirts and shorts that looked like they had just been picked out of the dryer. Today, dressed in their suits and polished shoes, they looked proud and professional.

As I looked at the students, I spotted Kelsey, a twenty-year-old undergraduate whom Dr. Starling and I had been helping the night before with her speech. She was seeking a summer internship, but she was nervous about presenting at the event. When I saw her face, I knew she was still scared. I could see the résumé paper that she was holding, shaking slightly in her hand as she sat waiting for her turn. At that moment, I decided to open the event with confidence.

"Welcome to the USD career fair!" I heard the words tumble out of my mouth and echo around the room. I addressed the audience while looking directly at Kelsey. I hoped to inspire her and help her realize that she could do a good job as well. As I spoke, the first ten students stood and lined up to get ready to deliver their sales pitches.

The woman beneath my suit was sleeping less than four hours a day. I was working, taking classes, completing the assignments for those classes, and leading SCMA initiatives. My mother and sister were still trying to let go of the past so they could fit into a new culture and discover their new identities and possibilities, but sometimes it seemed impossible for them to believe that new possibilities existed.

But at that moment, speaking before an audience for the very first time, I felt a new stalk growing out of the seed of confidence that Dr. Starling planted in me. That seed would continue to grow.

The following semester, in December 2003, I received a job offer of my own. I had been planning to graduate in December 2004, but this offer motivated me to push harder. I took a heavier course load the next spring and over the summer. In August 2004, three years after my mom and Ruba had arrived, I completed my MBA and made the next major move in my life. I would be travelling across the country to plant myself in a distant land I called, "Cannakty-kit." I didn't know what I'd find when I arrived. I wouldn't know a soul there. I couldn't even pronounce the name of the state. But I was on my way.

27 ⟩ *Home*

In the dream I'd had years and years before, I had climbed into the kitchen cabinet in my childhood home and entered a tunnel with a light at the end. When I stepped out onto the other side, I was standing in the middle of the most tranquil landscape. I didn't feel lost. I didn't feel confused. I didn't feel scared. I felt safe and content. I had never been to America, but these tree-lined rolling hills, covered in soft green grass that swayed in the breeze, looked to me like the place I imagined America to be— my intuition told me that this is where I was. I remember thinking, *I have arrived.* I stood there, hopeful and self-possessed, and knew I wanted to stay firmly in this breathtaking place. At last, the mysterious dream of my childhood became a reality.

It was September 2004. I opened my eyes before sunrise, before my alarm clock went off. I had hardly slept all night because of my excitement. I felt like a child waking up in anticipation of my birthday party. I had been waiting and preparing for this day for months since I had accepted the offer in December 2003. New opportunities were waiting for me; it felt like the first day of my new life.

I was intentional about every detail as I got dressed—my hair, makeup, the new and perfectly ironed navy suit and matching blue shirt that I prepared the night before. I put on a gold necklace with a pearl that Uncle Anton had given to me; I wore it for good luck. I wanted my appearance to perfectly match the new professional world I was taking my first step into. I wanted to look confident and capable. Mainly, I wanted my shiny exterior to hide the part of me that was still broken inside, filled with insecurities, heartbreak, and fears.

I left my studio apartment in Connecticut, bordering Upstate New York, with a big smile. I was filled with pride as I walked to the car I had rented. My excitement increased with every mile that I came closer to the IBM Somers, New York, office. The September sky was clear and blue; the sun was shining. I was driving and admiring my surroundings. On both sides of the narrow curvy streets I saw nothing but trees rising over hills. The leaves were beginning to turn yellow, red, and orange. I saw deer-crossing signs along the road and many little squirrels playing and running after each other. I was amused that these hilly roads, filled with the most picturesque natural beauty, were leading me into the most recognized high-tech company in the world.

I had been hired into IBM's Supply Chain Leadership Development Program. Each year, IBM chose eight MBA graduates from across the country to participate in the two-year rotational program. It was a competitive and prestigious program, and I was still amazed that I'd been one of the eight graduates selected. Within the two years, each participant would work four rotations with different departments, teams, and projects and move to different locations nationwide. On rare occasions, one might even be placed to work in a global rotation.

As I was admiring my surroundings, I found myself thinking about my mother and Ruba, whom I had left on their own in San Diego. Right before I left, my mother had started a day-care business in her new home. For the first time in her life, she decided to do something she was passionate about. There was nothing to hold her back. She had always loved children, but she felt she'd missed out on the joy in her own children's early years because of the abuse she was living with. She became the first woman business owner in our family. Ruba's life had also begun to improve. She was doing well in school and had her own car, so she could reliably get to school and work on her own. But, naturally, I was still worried about them. I wondered if it was too soon for me to leave them and whether they would be able to survive on their own. At the same time, I felt anxious that something might happen to them that could force me to sacrifice the new life I was beginning.

As I was thinking about them, a squirrel suddenly crossed the road in front of my car. I quickly hit the brakes, but I felt and heard a sound of something crack. "Oh no, I just killed a squirrel," I said out loud to myself. I pulled over to the side of the road and hurried out, hoping to find the squirrel alive. That little poor creature was alive, but with at least one foot injured. Crippled, it slowly moved to the other side of the road as I watched. I wondered if it would survive, but I knew that it would most likely not make it. I felt horrible and guilty, and I worried that the incident was a sign of bad luck on the first day of the new phase of my life.

To stop myself from thinking these limiting thoughts, I started thanking God. I thanked God for the opportunity I was about to experience. I thanked God over and over again until I arrived at IBM.

I parked the car and stepped out. I was greeted by the sounds of the birds chirping. The IBM offices were in the middle of the countryside, surrounded by hills and trees—a view of nature that looked like it belonged on a postcard.

The IBM Somers campus looked and felt completely futuristic to me. At the top of each of the five enormous white buildings, structures that looked like glass pyramids welcomed the sunlight inside. I witnessed a beautiful and stunning contrast between nature and technology. Internally, I was experiencing my own contrast of stepping out of the past and taking the first step into the future, as if I were crossing the border into a new world.

I had to take a moment to breathe before I began walking to one of the buildings. I did not know what to expect, but whatever it was, I felt internal assurance that it was going to be great. For the first time in my life, I felt like I had control over my own future. But for the first time, I also realized that this blessing came with a responsibility.

I walked inside the building and toward the reception area. The receptionist looked at me with a smile. I said, "I am Dima Ghawi, and I'm here to see Cindy Williams. She is expecting me, but I am a few minutes early." The receptionist asked me to sit down in the waiting area. As I waited, I observed every detail that surrounded me. I was amazed by the open space, the natural light flooding in from outside, and the crisp, clean feel of the contemporary furniture. I was even impressed by the graphic designs on the banners, the bold colors of blue, white, gray, and black. There was also bold modern art hanging on the walls. That entire space felt more like the reception area for a museum than for a Fortune 20 company.

Twenty or thirty people moved through the area, walking and talking in small groups of two or three and discussing paperwork that they were holding or rushing through the reception area and appearing to head to their desks or early meetings.

I could feel my heart jump with excitement as a woman walked toward me. She was in her mid-forties, blonde, and wearing a sharp black suit. "Hi, Dima, I'm Cindy," she said, and she extended her arm to shake my hand.

I stood up and smiled from ear to ear. "Hello, Cindy. It is so good to meet you."

She smiled back and said, "First, we'll go to my office, and then I'll walk you to the new-hire onboarding class." She waved at people who walked by us and said hello to them. Then she continued, "Today and tomorrow, you'll be here at the Somers office. After you're done with the onboarding class, you'll officially start your first rotation at the Southbury, Connecticut, office. You'll be working for the team that supports the sales order processing and fulfillment. I've already e-mailed you the address and name of the manager you'll be working for."

When we got to Cindy's office, she sat down and smiled. She leaned behind her desk and picked up a brown rectangular box and a white bag. She handed both packages to me and said, "Today is Christmas for you."

I opened the box and found an IBM ThinkPad inside. I had always wanted my own ThinkPad, but I could never afford to buy one. I looked at Cindy, hugged my ThinkPad, and smiled. Then I put it down on her desk and opened the white bag. In it, there was a black case with a blue, green, and red IBM logo at its center.

That experience did not just feel like Christmas. Arriving in this place felt like a homecoming.

The elevator door opened. I was wearing a new brown suit. It was September 2006. I had recently lost fifteen pounds, and I felt great about the way I looked and about life in general. That week, I celebrated my two-year anniversary with IBM. My department vice president was hosting IBM's global team for a leadership strategy meeting at the Research Triangle Park office in North Carolina, where I was now living and working.

As I stepped out of the elevator and into the usually quiet hallway, I heard many people talking. I heard voices of both women and men coming from the conference room, and, to my excitement, I heard many different accents. More than twenty-five team members whom I had worked with virtually for months were all in one place.

When I walked into the conference room, I felt like I was stepping into the United Nations. The room was well lit but had no windows. The projector was illuminating a screen with a slide welcoming everyone. On the right side of the room, team members were standing in groups and talking next to a table filled with silver urns full of hot coffee and trays full of bagels and fruit.

Everyone in the room was wearing a dark suit with an IBM badge clipped on. The conference room wooden table had many black IBM laptops placed in front of each seat. Several leather briefcases were on the floor next to chairs, but no one was sitting down yet. We still had twenty minutes until the meeting started.

I walked toward the table to put my briefcase and purse on one of the seats, and I started looking around and guessing who was who, comparing each individual in front of me with the images that I had in mind. As I looked around, a team member walked toward me with excitement. He looked to be in his fifties. He was wearing a fitted suit, which gave me the impression that he was from Europe. I thought he might be a German manager whom I'd been supporting on a project.

"Are you Dima?" he asked with a thick accent. "I'm Stefan."

"Stefan!" I said cheerfully, while opening my arms to give him a hug. After that, I met more and more people face-to-face, and I got to hug each team member. I laughed as I looked closely at their faces and guessed who they were, and in many cases, I made the wrong guesses.

At 8:30 a.m., after everyone had drunk at least one cup of coffee and had eaten something during our informal introductions, the meeting started. Everyone became serious and focused as we sat around at the conference table and listened to the vice president welcoming the global team. The most intelligent and strategic people that I have ever met surrounded me. I could not believe that I was here at the table.

Beneath my professional image, one that matched that of everyone sitting around me, I felt intimidated and overwhelmed. I wondered if people could see that little girl from Jordan who was terrified by the concept of the broken vase, the innocent girl who loved picking jasmine. Yet I also felt a powerful and deep sense of gratitude, knowing that my sacrifices, risks, long nights of hard work, fears and tears, and especially my cracked, broken shards of glass, put me at this table, with these people, playing an active role in planning global strategic initiatives that would influence thousands of employees' lives. I could tell that that my efforts were appreciated by my colleagues, that people listened when I spoke, and that my words and ideas had value.

That morning, in the conference room with my professional peers from near and far, I felt at home, surrounded by my people. These IBMers from all over the world—my coworkers, mentors, teachers—they were my community. For the first time in my life, I felt a sense of belonging and worth.

28) *New Heights*

In July 2007, I was visiting my mother in San Diego when my manager called my cell phone. "Are you interested in moving to Japan?" he asked. "The leadership team is discussing the possibility of sending you on an international assignment."

International assignments were rare and prestigious, so without thinking, I responded, "Yes! Of course—I would love to move to Japan."

Six months later, on January 2, 2008, I flew to Narita Airport. My apartment was on the thirtieth floor with a view of Tokyo Bay on the east and Mount Fuji on the west. At sunrise, I watched the fishing boats coming back to the bay, and at sunset, on the clearest days, I could see Mount Fuji in the distance.

I relocated to Japan to work with an executive manager in driving process improvements; I was also there to help enhance the overall communication between IBM's Japanese and American procurement teams. This opportunity provided me with financial security for the first time in my life. IBM paid for my apartment and utilities, and I earned a salary in both Japan and the United States. I could finally start paying off debts I had accumulated while taking care of my mother and sister and completing my MBA. It felt as if God were giving me long-awaited relief.

My first day in the office, I was excited to meet my new manager, Steve, who had moved to Japan a year before I had. We spoke on the phone a few times in the six months leading up to my move. I had asked him, among many preliminary questions, "Do you have any advice about how I should interact with the Japanese team so I can hit the ground running?"

Without hesitation, he answered, "Just be yourself."

Being "myself" as a professional leader had been a learning process. When I had been insecure and timid, Dr. Starling put me on the path and taught me the fundamentals of a skilled leadership style: I was efficient and to the point, and my direct nature had become more fine-tuned over the years. This style had won me recognition, promotions, and awards, including the position in Japan.

"I can do that," I'd cheerfully responded to Steve over the phone. I felt ready to bring my skills to the table.

The language, the customs, my manager, and my team—everything was new to me. I had experienced culture shock when I first left Jordan, and I'd adapted. So I expected that I would adapt quickly and easily in Japan.

One of the first things I noticed is that Steve easily stood out from others in the Hakozaki office. In a building that housed nine thousand IBM employees, he was the only African American. He was also the epitome of a successful American executive: he had a tall, athletic build; he wore well-groomed, formal black suits with crisp blue ties; and he had a wide, expressive, and toothy smile. Once we were standing face-to-face, he greeted me with a warm, high-spirited hug and welcomed me to his team. He exuded confidence, independence, and a bold streak.

In comparison, the three hundred Japanese team members who worked in the department, including the eighty whom he directly managed, were all slim bodied and of an average height. They were polite, reserved, and even muted during meetings. This was very different from the dynamic, sometimes heated round-table discussions I was used to in the United States, and I had a lot of trouble reading the personalities and situations. In my previous competitive, corporate environment, I was used to more aggressive personalities and to vocalizing opinions and ideas in a more direct manner.

Another thing I noticed right away is that I stood out. Apart from Steve, I was the only other American in our department, and more often than not, I was the only woman in an ocean of men in dark suits. In addition to being one of the few females, I was younger than most of my colleagues, and I was single. For someone in a leadership position, all of these facts were outside the Japanese norm. I quickly faced challenges I had not anticipated.

First, I was unfamiliar with the rituals, traditions, and the distinct set of manners that were highly regarded in their culture; I soon found out that this also applied in their executive world. The unspoken expectation—which I did not understand initially—was that good leaders should be reserved and patient in their approach with team members, but I had an exuberant personality. I was also there, in part, to help the Japanese team meet deadlines they were not meeting. I entered this role with confidence and assertiveness that was perfectly acceptable, and even desirable, in American offices. I comfortably spoke up in meetings and asked team members I was leading to also offer their opinions. In response, the Japanese teams looked at me in silence, waiting for someone senior to speak up on their behalf.

My second challenge hit me at a more personal and emotional level. I'd left Jordan eleven years earlier. In Japan, I saw almost immediately that I'd entered into another paternalistic culture. Whether in or out of the office, women were held to a confining and demeaning set of expectations. I met a pregnant woman who was completely distraught that she would be returning to work after having her child, because it would indicate that her husband could not take care of his family and she would be looked down on. I met another woman who berated herself because she was in her forties and still single. She confessed to me that every night, she went home and drank herself into tears because she felt so judged and inadequate. I also worked with women, though they were few compared to the number of men, who were wildly talented and smart but who constantly put themselves down in the office to placate their male colleagues.

I experienced complete culture shock. What I'd learned in the United States—to be self-assured and direct—was causing me conflict. Japanese corporate culture did not value the qualities that had helped me thrive up to that point. Furthermore, as a woman, I was met with even greater skepticism, and learning about the experiences of the women I spoke with had triggered my emotions. Unexpectedly, I was reliving my own traumas related to becoming an autonomous woman. If I hadn't fit the mold in Jordan, I really did not fit the mold in Japan.

The fact that my mere presence and leadership style seemed to be obstacles to successfully engaging my team, and the fact that I was suddenly in a male-dominated culture again after so many years, together with my new and treasured sense of security, shook me fundamentally. I experienced a new type of anxiety—I was constantly and deeply fearful that something would happen to take my material security away from me. I was hyperaware that what had been given to me could vanish in an instant. My fear and anxiety became my main motivators.

As I tried to hold my teams accountable to the ambitious project timelines and drive process improvements using the approaches I'd learned, my method was not well received. The team resisted my style. They would not directly address their issues or concerns to me, but within a few months, they started ignoring my strategies and the changes I was trying to implement.

To prove my worth and capability—to my superiors in the

United States, to myself, and to my new Japanese colleagues—
and to maintain the privileges I was living with, I dug in harder.
When none of the tactics I was familiar with were working, instead of trying new approaches, I relied more intensely on the
same methods, telling myself that I must not be performing them
well enough. I became fixated on project deliverables, timelines,
and target dates, fearful that my managers in the States were
worrying about the same issues. I organized more meetings. I as-
signed specific tasks with hard deadlines to team members. I e-
mailed them reminders, believing this was a helpful, effective approach, but also knowing it would force them to be as aware of
the deadlines as I was. During my meetings, everyone sat quietly,
staring blankly; eventually, many stopped attending.

When I attended someone else's meetings, I sat looking at my
colleagues, trying to capture any pieces of information I could
translate for myself. During brief pauses in the conversation, I
asked, "Can you please translate to English?"

To my surprise, the men would continue speaking in Japanese,
and at the end of the meeting, someone would provide me with a
few brief sentences in English that summarized the entire discussion. Often, the meeting summary would be unclear, or I would
realize that, based on prior projects, the American executive
team would challenge their conclusions. But by the time someone
shared the summary with me, it was the end of the meeting and
too late to contribute to the decision.

Months after I moved to Tokyo, an interpreter who always ac-
companied one of the senior executives approached me after a
particularly difficult meeting and said, "Dima-san, do you realize what you are doing?"

I stopped gathering my papers and looked at her. "No, I do
not," I answered, "but I always feel something strange is going on
in these meetings that I can't explain. What am I doing?" I asked.
By this point, I felt deflated and bewildered.

She explained, "The seat facing the door is traditionally reserved for the most important person in the room. In every meeting, when the team walks in, you are always early, and you are always sitting in the chair facing the door."

I was stunned and embarrassed. "I had no idea!" I said, and I
thanked her for telling me.

I had read books about Japanese culture to prepare myself for
this assignment. They all noted the importance of being on time
for meetings, so I was intentionally early, but none of my books
specified that there was an etiquette about where to sit in a conference room. Without realizing it, I had been insulting my team
and clients on a regular basis, unintentionally challenging the
power hierarchy and sending the message that I was either arro-
gant or ignorant. I wondered in what other ways I had been unintentionally insulting people.

I started befriending a few of the interpreters who were as-
signed to the top executives. I spoke to them and tried to learn
more about the culture I'd entered into. I learned that my colleagues believed they should not speak openly about their own
accomplishments, skills, or strengths, that this was considered
to be self-promotion; I learned that in the presence of leadership,
they believed it was respectful to let managers speak for them instead of offering their own opinions. I learned that, in their eyes,
my leadership style had seemed too direct and aggressive.

Japanese culture is complex. In spite of my preparation, I was
resisting the Japanese model of leadership. I was relying on the
American model out of a sense of self-protection, but I couldn't
understand exactly why. Eventually, and not without a struggle, I
realized I was stuck in an emotional response. I had worked hard
to recognize and accept my emerging identity after I left Jordan,
and now I *loved* my American identity. This new environment reminded me in a visceral way of my upbringing. I didn't want to go
back to being quiet and submissive.

My resistance to change came in part from ego and in part from appreciating the direct communication and leadership style. But I mainly resisted changing because I did not want to mold myself into someone I was not. My emotional response was standing in my way; I couldn't see that I wasn't being a good leader.

Not long after the interpreter first approached me, I reached a breaking point. I knew this experience could ruin my career if I didn't make changes. I spoke with my mentor in North Carolina, who said to me, "Dima, what matters is not *what* you do. What matters is *how* you do it."

I slowly started to realize that if I were going to succeed in this assignment, I had to adapt to the business culture I was in. This experience challenged me to evolve and expand my leadership capabilities by learning how to lead across cultures, building the essential skills to influence teams globally. And I had to do this without sacrificing the strong values I'd created for myself, or my self-identify. That was the *real* opportunity that had been presented to me the day I received the phone call asking if I wanted to go to Japan; it just took a long time to recognize.

29 The Last Exchange

One day in mid-March 2008 when I was meeting with Steve, I noticed a pile of brightly colored pamphlets about Mount Fuji stacked on the left side of his desk. He saw me eyeing them.

"I want to share a vision that I have," Steve began. "I'd like to plan a team-building activity over the summer." He picked up one of the pamphlets and handed it to me, then continued: "Wouldn't it be a great idea for our team to climb Mount Fuji together?"

As I held the pamphlet and looked at it, my heart started beating fast. Not only did I have an extreme fear of heights, but also, looking at the picture of the enormous mountain on the pamphlet, I remembered reading an article about the high levels of seismic activity under the volcano, raising concern about a future eruption. I had absolutely no desire to climb this ticking lava bomb.

"You're IN, right?" Steve asked, looking directly into my eyes.

I don't know how it happened, but I heard myself reply, "Yes! I can do it!"

Initially, about fifteen people were interested in the hike. As August neared, one by one, people began to change their minds, concerned about the intensity of the physical activity. When the week of the hike arrived, only four of us remained: Steve, Moto-san, Okubo-san, and me. Moto-san was in his sixties, and he had been with IBM his entire career. Okubo-san was an ambitious man with a goal of becoming an executive manager in the future. Both men had resisted my leadership in the office.

The first day, we met early in the morning at a train station in the middle of Tokyo. The four of us were energized and ready for our adventure. We were going to begin our ascent from the fifth station, located at the middle of the mountain, up to the tenth and final station, located at the peak. After hours on multiple train and bus rides, we arrived at the fifth station. Each of us was weighed down by backpacks filled with extra layers of clothing, oxygen bottles, energy bars, and bottles of water. The sun was shining and the sky was clear blue, but we were in hot, dense, humid August air and were looking forward to the temperature dropping as we ascended the mountain.

Before we began, Steve turned toward us, grinning, and said, "Let's have fun with this. Let's see who gets to the top first." Before we could comprehend what he meant, Steve put in his headphones, turned his music up, and left us standing there as he started his hike up the mountain. I looked up at the towering volcano ahead of us. It seemed one hundred times larger than I'd imagined.

At that moment, I wanted to turn around and get back on the bus as it was leaving the mountain. Moto-san, Okubo-san, and I were left with a daunting adventure ahead. I did not think I had the experience or skills to climb the mountain. But I already felt like I was failing in so many ways during my time in Japan, so I was determined to prove to myself that I was capable of climbing this mountain and capable of keeping up with my Japanese teammates.

I put one foot in front of the other, and so did Moto-san and Okubo-san. Slowly, we began making progress together. Moto-san was twice my age, but he was stronger and faster than I was. I pushed myself to keep up with them. I did not want to fall behind—both because I wanted to show myself I could keep up and because I didn't want to slow my team members down.

Two hours in, my muscles began to ache. As the slope became steeper and the rocks increased in size, it took more energy to climb. My feet throbbed and my legs ached. My shoulders hurt from carrying my backpack, and my arms grew sore from climbing the towering rocks.

When we reached the sixth station, we stopped at a concession stand and purchased Bento boxes with fish and rice. I looked around as I ate, and I gained a new appreciation for the number of families that included older adults and little children who were all making the same strenuous hike. They were making a pilgrimage to the highest Shinto temple at the tenth station, and their perseverance and dedication humbled me.

As we started hiking to the seventh station, I began walking slower and lagging behind. Whatever power dynamic had existed between the three of us had dissolved completely. Instead of thinking of myself as someone who was on a hike with two men who had resisted my leadership in the office, I thought of myself as someone who needed to fully trust the two men I was with, not just on this hike but also in the office. Okubo-san and Moto-san slowed down when I slowed down. They took turns holding my backpack as we traversed enormous boulders. I also took turns holding their packs and giving them a hand over challenging passes.

I couldn't keep up with them on the mountain anymore, even doing the best that I could, and it began to occur to me that maybe they and all of the Japanese team members I was working with were also doing the best they could do on our projects. I wondered what would happen if I stopped trying to rely so force-

fully on my Western approach of assertiveness and instead tried
to rely on my ability to trust that my team wanted to succeed as
much as I did.

The oxygen level decreased as we continued up, and it became
difficult to breathe. Our lungs tightened as we struggled to in-
hale a full breath. Walking a few yards could take ten minutes or
more as we trudged up the steep incline, breathing heavily. Sometimes it felt as if we were tethered to one spot, unable to walk
without resistance. I saw Okubo-san stop completely on the burgundy volcanic rock and try to take a full breath while he wiped
sweat from his brow. We had discussed the symptoms of altitude
sickness as we were preparing for the hike, but now we were experiencing them.

We still had a two-hour climb before we would get to the
eighth station, where we were looking forward to having a warm
meal at the lodge. But by this time, we had no energy, so we
stopped to rest.

Sunset was approaching; we sat on a bench inhaling oxygen
from Moto-san's oxygen bottle. I looked around at the ground,
taking in the fact that we were so high up that there was no longer any growth on the mountain. Moto-san and Okubo-san began commenting on the view. I could tell from their voices that
they were in awe. "Ahhh . . . Dima-san, look up," they were saying. "Look at the changing colors of the sky. We are sitting right
in the sunset, as if we are a part of it."

"I don't want to look," I told them. "I'm afraid I won't be able
to keep going if I know how high up we are."

"Dima-san, you will not regret it if you look," Moto-san
promised.

I decided it was time to work up the courage to look outward.
I had intentionally climbed the entire way without turning back
or looking down the slope. I closed my eyes, took a deep breath,

lifted my chin, opened my eyes, and scanned my surroundings, trying to see the valley below and looking down the mountain as far as my eye could see.

Around us, a sunset of orange, red, and purple painted the most stunning canvas. When I let my eyes drift down the mountainside, I realized we were completely above the clouds, which hid the ordinary world well below us. I laughed out loud and breathed in the cold mountain air. "Arigato," I said, bowing my head to Moto-san and Okubo-san. "Thank you for convincing me to experience this gorgeous view."

The two men nodded simply and seemed to smile with their eyes.

It was clear to all of us by then, without having to say it, that if we worked together, we would stay safe and reach our destination. I knew that I could not complete the hike without their help.

As I was taking in the view, I thought of my mother and sister. After they'd escaped Jordan and moved to California, we focused on our physical, emotional, and financial well-being. Apart from the nightly ritual of counting our bodies out loud and celebrating small wins with bottles of sparkling wine, we didn't make time to look away and just experience the colors of our lives or the changing distances and views, as I had just allowed myself to do.

This was out of necessity; we were in a reactive mode, putting all of our energy into surviving. It was almost impossible to stop and experience any moment. Now, on this mountain, I realized I was in a very different place in my life. It was time for me to adopt a different mind-set, not just toward my personal life but also toward my professional life.

With the sun disappearing beneath the layer of clouds, the sky became darker, and the evening became chilly. Moto-san, Okubo-san, and I were eager to reach the warmth of the lodge and were even more eager to have a hearty dinner. We pressed on, step by painful step, and continued up the volcano, motivated by the image of a big bowl of hot miso soup and steamed rice.

We reached the eighth station around 9:30 p.m. When we arrived, we immediately went to the simple, wooden lodge to get some nourishment. As soon as we entered the building, Steve appeared out of nowhere. He was waiting in anticipation for our arrival.

I asked, "How is dinner? We are starving!"

Steve replied, "Dinner was great. They served hot miso soup, steamed rice, dried fish, and hot green tea. But . . ." As he continued, the expression on his face changed, as if he realized for the first time what he was about to say and how it would hit me. "The kitchen closed thirty minutes ago." My face fell.

Moto-san, Okubo-san, and I were freezing, exhausted, and starving. Between us, we had several energy bars left. We found a corner to sit in. Moto-san pulled some of the bars from his backpack for us to share.

The lodge was a one-story building, and inside was a large, open room where everyone slept. The communal space had a colorful array of mismatched quilts and blankets, and small cots lined the floor. Each hiking group was allocated a small area within the room to share. Steve, Moto-san, Okubo-san, and I slept side by side on an orange quilt that felt smaller than a queen-sized bed. We were in a cramped corner, with each of our backpacks hanging on metal hooks above our heads. We did not have the energy to change into clean clothes and decided to keep wearing the same sweaty, smelly clothes that we'd hiked in all day.

At 10:00 p.m., the lodge staff turned off the lights, indicating that everyone should stop chatting and go to sleep. Even in these uncomfortable conditions, we immediately fell asleep.

Less than four hours later, we woke to the sound of the banging of a gong. Soon after, someone turned on all the lights. The goal was to wake everyone up to continue the climb in order to reach the top of the mountain before sunrise. As I opened my eyes, I could feel that my whole body was sore. My legs were tight, and my feet ached from the previous day's journey. Moto-san, Okubo-san, and Steve were also still half asleep.

"How about we just watch the sunrise from this station and sleep for a couple more hours?" I asked, feeling certain that the men would want to get to the top. To my surprise, the three of them immediately agreed, and we each went back to sleep.

The four of us woke up again at 4:00 a.m., packed up our belongings, filled our thermoses with tea, and headed outside into the dark. In the freezing cold air, we sat next to each other on a big rock, drinking hot green tea. We were bundled up in hats and warm layers but still needed to stay close to each other to keep warm. As I sipped my tea, I felt it heat my insides. Outside, I could see steam rising from our thermoses at the same time that I could see our breath blow out of our mouths; the cold breath and hot steam mingled in a strange dance until they vanished into the air. We were each brimming with anticipation for this exquisite gift from nature, a reward for our long, difficult climb. In a brief matter of minutes, the dark turned to light, and we were greeted by a spectacular pink sunrise, unlike any I had ever witnessed.

When we reached the peak at 7:30 in the morning, Steve, who had arrived before us, was waiting. Moto-san and Okubo-san started bowing toward Steve, toward me, and toward each other to respectfully show appreciation for making it to the top.

"Forget about the bow," I said. "I want to give you both a big American hug." I leaned in, hugged them, and thanked them for being amazing team members whom I could trust and respect.

The two traditional Japanese men stood rigidly with their arms to their sides, too uncomfortable to hug me back. But they managed to smile, with their mouths open and their teeth showing, a rare surprise. They even laughed out loud with me.

Breaking the cultural norm felt right in that moment; in doing so, I didn't feel intimidated or worried that I would unintentionally offend my team members. We were each celebrating the accomplishment we'd achieved together, just in our own ways.

On the mountain, I had no choice except to return to the absolute basics of my humanity, to admit my own weaknesses when I needed to, and to adapt as needed. In turn, I became more adaptable as a leader and a less fearful human being; whatever anxiety I'd fostered when I arrived in Japan, I let go of on that day.

I knew that once I went back to the office, everything would be smoother between my teammates and me. My Japanese colleagues were hard workers, but they were also oriented to working at a much slower pace and were uncomfortable with change. But I realized that they were valuable contributors in their own traditional ways. I became deliberate in connecting with them and understanding their priorities. I trusted that instead of focusing on results first, if I was patient and focused on human connections and trust, the results would follow. This lesson, learned after many months of fighting against it, became the foundation of my leadership style, not just in Japan but also across the globe.

At the top of Mount Fuji, we stopped at the famous post office where hikers and pilgrims mail their loved ones postcards to share that they made it to the peak. I picked out a postcard. I wanted to send it to my mother and Ruba, but I didn't have their addresses with me, so I addressed it to myself and mailed it to my apartment in Tokyo. I wrote on the back, "I did it!" I had evolved as a leader and become a citizen of the world.

Before Steve, Moto-san, and Okubo-san began to hike down the mountain, I visited the crater at the center of the peak. Standing at the edge of the crater, I took a few minutes to reflect on my family. Who would have predicted, I wondered—when I was born and my grandfather wished that I would die because I was a girl, when my grandmother taught me about living with the perfect glass vase, when my husband warned me that I would not make it on my own and would beg like a dog to go back to him, and when my father threatened to make me minced meat—that I would achieve a life beyond my wildest dreams, beyond what I thought was possible or allowed for a woman with my background?

Who would have predicted that my mother would begin a child-care service in her home that enabled her to become the first female business owner in our family, to start earning a modest income so she could become financially stable, to slowly start rebuilding her savings, and to live in a beautiful home in a safe neighborhood, attaining independence that extended far beyond driving a car?

And who would have predicted that Ruba would step onto the path toward earning her bachelor's degree, boosting her confidence and building her own dream to one day achieve both a master's and a PhD?

Each one of us was climbing her own challenging and amazing mountain.

The crater was an enormous circle that was once filled with bright, bubbling orange lava. Many people were gathered around its diameter. In spite of my pride over making the ascent, I knew that my fear that the dormant volcano could erupt reflected my deepest personal fear. My father had been a dormant presence in our lives, and it was impossible not to wonder if he would become an active threat at some point.

I looked into the crater and breathed in deeply. The sun warmed my bare arms at the same time as the mountain air made my cheeks feel cool; it was a strange dual sensation. I considered my earlier determination to adopt a new mind-set. The difference now, I told myself, is that if he erupts, we have the tools. The three of us have acquired the resources, confidence, tight bonds, extended network, and the knowledge and emotional strength to stand up for ourselves. I told myself this: *Dima, don't you forget it*. It was only a matter of time before I would need to rely on a few of these tools.

I'm like many girls: growing up, I wanted to be my father's daughter, a daddy's girl. In October 2011, just over two years after I returned to North Carolina from Japan, my father sent me a friend request on Facebook.

I panicked when I saw the invitation. I immediately worried that he may have searched me out online and in other ways, learning about my employment and my home address. I was also worried about my mother and Ruba, who had become a mother five months earlier, ushering the first grandchild and next generation into our family. I didn't want to endanger any of us.

Instead of accepting his request, the next day I sent him a one-sentence message wishing him well. He responded in Arabic, thanking me and asking to hear more from me. Over the course of three months, we sent each other a few messages; mine were always written in English, and his were always written in Arabic.

To one of his early messages, I responded, "Life is like a dream. We start in one place and end in another." I told him, "I'm trying to move forward. Even though I am still deeply hurt and sad."

To my surprise, he responded in a loving way, one that sounded completely out of character for the man I had grown up with. He wrote, "You are the dearest person to me in this universe, and even beyond." Then he wrote more. He wrote that he was doing well. He wrote about his health issues, his retirement from the government, the school clinic he was working in, and the healthy state of his finances. "I would be happy if you respond with more messages," he said. He signed it, "Your Dad."

This was his longest correspondence. Though he'd written a lot, everything was on the surface, and I felt uneasy. *Was this conversation initiated out of love or revenge? Was I safe?* I genuinely did not know. I responded with surface information. I told him I was doing well professionally and that I was happy.

Again, he responded in a way that was unfamiliar to me. "I'm happy to hear your good news," he wrote. "I've been thirsty for it." This language and his outpouring of affection made me feel as if I were exchanging notes with a stranger. And in fact, I realized that after more than ten years, he was a stranger to me.

He didn't tell me about his second wife, but we'd heard about her through extended community members. Instead, he told me about the two-story house he'd built; he said it was a beautiful home in a nice area. "There is a large, healthy garden that has a lot of roses and trees and vines," he shared.

Meanwhile, I also knew that after fighting my mother for the ownership of our home after she had filed for divorce, he had ultimately abandoned the house I'd grown up in. We'd heard that his wife had been one of his longtime patients and that two months after my parents' divorce was final, they'd married and moved into her home. He'd taken all of the furniture with him, leaving nothing. He had even taken the toilets out of the bathrooms before he left our home to rot. In 2008, while I was in Tokyo, my brother had visited Jordan in secret. He'd seen with his own eyes that the interior walls of our home were crumbling. He took photos of the destruction and decay, including torn and discarded family photos and broken glass scattered on the floors in every room; the place where I'd grown up had become a looted shell of a home.

In all of my father's messages, the only hint of the past was this one sentence: "I love my work because it keeps me preoccupied from thinking about sadness in life."

I think that was the line that broke me.

I had been having these polite exchanges with him, but I felt nervous and guarded. If we were going to communicate, I didn't want to talk about his rose garden. I wanted to talk openly about what happened and how he felt about it after all these years. If we could do that—if I could sense and really *believe* he had experienced an internal shift, then I would have been happy to know about the details of his life. Then I might have felt safe asking and knowing more.

From all of his messages, I got the sense that he didn't want me to pity him. I think he wanted me to believe that he was doing okay, on the inside and out—that our family leaving had not broken him as a man. But my father had told me many stories in the past. *Then*, I had believed them all. *Now*, I didn't believe my father's story so completely.

I sent him a lengthy response, hoping to get closer to the truth; if he couldn't share how he'd really felt and how it had really impacted him, I could share my truth:

> For years now, I have been focusing on releasing the pains of the past and working really hard to forgive you. . . . I realize that you tried in your own way to be a good Father, based on the knowledge and resources you had.

Then, I asked him for something I knew might surprise and upset him:

It is good that you are currently surrounded by people that you like, that you have a nice home, hobbies and activities in your life, and that you are busy working. It is also good that you are sharing this information with me in your notes, but what I need is healing.

In order for me to achieve that, I need your apology. Apology for all the tears that I cried in my life because of your controlling behavior, apology for the sadness that resulted from your selfish actions, apology for making me feel alone and helpless in this life when I needed you the most, apology for telling me that I was bringing shame to you and the family, apology for destroying my engagement year, apology for making me take responsibility for an entire family when I was only twenty-four years old because you gave up on all of us, apology for all the screaming and yelling and the fear that you planted in my heart . . . just a pure sincere apology. . . . You now have the chance to make it up and fix this. It is all in your hands.

For two days after I hit "send," I felt nauseous and could not leave my home. In my community, a child does not ask an elder for an apology; this is incredibly insulting and disrespectful. But I wasn't in the Middle East anymore, and I absolutely needed to know that he had reflected and that he realized we both needed to grow and evolve if we were going to have a relationship. I needed to know that he wasn't a volcano lying dormant, ready to erupt at any time.

He responded with silence.

I had the answers to my questions, and this was our last exchange.

30 All the Beautiful Shards of Glass

It is 2014, and I've been working with IBM as talent development manager in its new Technology Center in Baton Rouge, Louisiana, for one year. I've been invited to speak about an idea worth spreading at Louisiana State University at an event called TEDxLSU. TEDx is a localized offshoot of the international TED Talks.

I've drafted three speeches over four months. The drafts narrate my global leadership experiences over the past eleven years and insights about cross-cultural business understanding. They include funny stories and visuals about mistakes I made while working in Japan, my projects with the United Nations in South Africa, and my experiences leading teams and training managers across various countries. After completing every draft, reading and rereading, and practicing each one, I feel disconnected from everything I've written. I keep feeling that I should talk about something else, but I do not know what it is.

On a call with my friend Donna, I express my frustration. "The TEDx event is in less than a month, and I still do not have a speech; what am I am going to do? The rehearsals are coming up and I am going to embarrass myself."

Donna and I met at IBM in March 2009 in Raleigh after I

moved back from Japan, and we became instant friends. She became a mentor to me. As someone I look up to and trust, she
always provides me with wise guidance. "Why don't you share
your grandmother's story about the broken vase, the one you
once told me?"

I immediately respond, "I can't. It is too personal. I just moved
to Louisiana less than a year ago. What if the new community
judges me? Who would want to hear that story anyway?"

Just like Dr. Startling had been, Donna is persistent. Every time
I start writing a new speech about global business and cultural
understanding, she directs me back to the vase story. She helps
me daily; every evening after work, I call her around 6:30 p.m.
and we talk for hours. I start writing a fourth speech, focusing on
the vase, but I avoid sharing details, especially about the consequences of shattering the vase. Donna keeps saying, "People will
want to know. You have to give more details."

On every call, I ask, "Are you sure that it is a good idea to
share the broken vase story?"

Every time, she patiently assures me, "Yes. The audience will
love it." Without Donna, I would have most likely given another
business presentation and never had the courage to share my
story on the stage.

I decide to take the week off before the TEDx event so I can focus on finishing my speech and practicing. On my last day in the
office, I'm working on closing urgent action items and getting myself caught up before my vacation, when the receptionist calls to
tell me there are four women from a local nonprofit in the lobby
waiting to meet with me.

"I thought I requested that we reschedule that meeting," I say.
To my horror, I realize I either hadn't or there has been a miscom-
munication. As the face of IBM in the community, I know I need
to go forward with the meeting. I go out to greet the small group
and bring them into the conference room.

After meeting for an hour, one of the women requests that we schedule a follow-up meeting the next week. I tell her, "I'll be out of the office. I'm preparing for a TEDx talk I'm scheduled to give at LSU."

The woman says, "Oh, my best friend helped out with Bill Gates's TED talk. Would you like me to connect you with him?"

Here I had been resisting meeting with this group, but the universe has another plan. I think, how often does someone meet a person who has worked with Bill Gates, and on a speech of all things?

"Of course! That would be amazing," I answer.

She connects me to Barry over e-mail, and he speaks with me over the phone three times that week, about an hour each time. My speech includes a PowerPoint presentation, and he tells me to get rid of it. He suggests that I should use only a vase as my tool for communicating with the audience.

I am completely uncomfortable and, more than once, I begin crying on the phone with this total stranger. "The audience just needs you and the vase," he assures me, "nothing else." Then he repeats, "Just you and the vase."

The day before the talk, March 29, I say, "Barry, I'm afraid I'm going to forget my speech. I'm afraid I'm going to embarrass myself. I'm just going to read the speech to the audience. I am so thankful for your help, but I can't perform it the way you're teaching me."

He says firmly, "No! You are *not* going to read that speech. This is your story. Just stand there and share it with the world. Look at the audience and inspire them with your journey." He is firm.

The same day, my mother flies in from San Diego to Baton Rouge. The entire night, I practice the speech with Donna and her sister, who have both flown in from Raleigh to cheer me on. As I practice, my mother looks tense and uncomfortable. I know she is worried about me sharing our family's story and our deepest wounds. This makes me feel even more anxious and nervous.

While I've been preparing my speech, Ruba has been wrapping up her spring semester of graduate school, working full-time, and caring for her son, Alex.

My mother has been managing her home child-care business for twelve years at this point, continuing to educate herself by becoming Montessori certified and completing various other courses and certifications in child development. Her business has grown to the point that she has a small staff. My nephew, Alex, is one of the lucky children who stays in his Tata's care, laughing together, singing songs she showers her children with, absorbing her love, creativity, and the fresh-cooked meals she prepares each day. She's taken time off to be here with me for the TEDx event.

The day of the event, I wake up thinking of many "what-ifs." I'm especially worried that I won't be able to breathe due to stage fright. I rub essential oils on my chest: lavender and rose to calm my nerves and peppermint and lime to help me breathe. When I walk into the green room, I smell like a flower garden. The room is crowded with tables of drinks, food, swag bags, and people. Some of the speakers are conversing and laughing with volunteers, while other speakers pace in a small area, gripping note cards and moving their lips while practicing their speeches in silence.

Two conflicting feelings have battled inside me for weeks. I am terrified to stand on that stage and deliver the speech, but also, deep inside, something is pushing me, telling me that the story is ready to come out. For the last weeks, I have been visualizing with my speaking coach, Cathy, sometimes daily. We keep repeating a specific visual: I hear my name being announced. I walk onto the stage, look at the audience, deliver the speech, and then walk off the stage.

I'm the closing speaker, and as the time creeps nearer, I feel more and more anxious. I leave the green room and walk down a dark hallway, checking each doorknob for an open and empty room until I find a small dressing room. I walk in and close the door behind me. I take off my white jacket, sit at the small chair, look at myself in the mirror, and panic. *What am I doing giving this speech? Oh GOD. I should've just presented about a business topic. What if the audience judges me? What if they do not relate?* Negative thoughts keep playing in my mind.

I still have two hours. I call Cathy over Skype and practice the speech with her again and again. She gives me guidance on my voice, tone, the speed, and my body language, up until the last minute.

"Do you think giving this speech is a good idea?" I ask her, seriously.

For the millionth time, Cathy patiently gives me the same answer as Donna, "Yes, Dima, the audience will love it."

Still, I don't know if I'm ready to speak authentically about my past and how it propelled me into the present. I am terrified of standing in front of four hundred strangers in a theater and also in front of a virtual, global audience, being totally vulnerable to judgments about the deepest pain in my life.

As we're practicing, Cathy says, "Dima, remember, your speech, your story—it is no longer about you. It is about the people who will hear it and become motivated to shatter their own vase."

Her words startle me. I realize that she is right, and that Donna and Barry had also been trying to say the same thing all along. Cathy's words get the message across to me. Not only do I realize that she is right; I also know I *want* people to benefit from hearing about my experience; I want my story to help others. I am still nervous, but I suddenly have a defined purpose for walking onto the stage and delivering the words that are about to come out of my mouth.

I look at my cell phone to check the time. It is fifteen minutes until my turn. I hear someone in the hallway ask, "Where is Dima?" I open the door and find two young volunteers, college students dressed in the black TEDx T-shirts and dark blue jeans. One of them looks at me, smiles, and says, "Your talk is next. Please follow me."

When the moment arrives, my heart beats faster and faster. I feel guided by an intuition that gives me no choice—I am compelled to take this risk. It seems that the story is ready to come out, and I am just a medium. I show up and deliver the message.

Onstage, I stand in the middle of the red round circle on the floor. Bright, hot spotlights point at me. I look at the audience, though I cannot make faces out beyond the first two rows. The words start coming out of my mouth. I have fifteen minutes to deliver a message that has been developing for months, but really over my lifetime. For the first time ever, I open myself up and share the essence of my being—the shame, the fear, the death threats, and the learned beliefs and events that have been shattering me internally since the day Tata taught me about the vase.

As I speak, I hold a vase that represents the limitations I experienced throughout my life. But I also talk about my transformation. At the end of the talk, without an ounce of hesitation, I move my two hands apart and let the vase drop. It smashes into what seems like a million pieces. It feels like the world has stopped for a millisecond. I hear the crash on the wood beneath my feet. I feel the audience members in the front rows flinch. I hear the air seep out of the room for a minute, until everyone exhales—then I hear clapping and cheering.

I remember that my mom is somewhere in this crowd. Even

though I can't see her, I am overjoyed that she is here, seeing and hearing this audience's reaction, firsthand.

I feel liberated. I am no longer the young woman who is wearing a suit on the outside, but hiding a different self beneath, as I had been the first time I took a stage as a student at USD.

After the talk, I see my mother. She hugs me and says, "Dima, you were great. I am happy that you shattered your vase and helped me to shatter mine."

During the reception that evening, when I introduce her to one person after another, I say, "This is my mom, and she also shattered her vase."

Apart from the brief period of Facebook messages, not a single one of us—my mother, Uncle Anton, Auntie Nadia, Waseem, Ruba, me, and even his own cousin Auntie Mariam—has spoken to my father since my mother and sister escaped years ago; this was when we all left him for good. I have accepted what my experience was; I have accepted that my father had his own vase to protect, but I don't accept that I have to participate in the cycle any longer.

Every teardrop of the past finally has a clear purpose. After delivering my message to that audience, I know my story is meant to inspire and heal others. The TEDx stage is just the beginning.

EPILOGUE

2017

In September 2014, my ten-year anniversary with IBM and six months after I gave my first TEDx talk, Ruba and her then three-year-old son, Alex, flew from San Diego to Baton Rouge for a visit. By then, I'd given similar speeches on a few different occasions, each time shattering a new vase. After these speeches, to commemorate the experiences, I collected shards of the clear glass and put them in the ceramic bowl I'd purchased in Jordan for myself after I first graduated. I placed the bowl filled with broken glass in the center on the coffee table at my home. So here was this object, mixing traditional Middle Eastern images with a modern style, and it contained broken glass—souvenirs of breaking away from the past, breaking my silence, and becoming empowered.

Ruba and Alex arrived in the mid-afternoon. I picked them up from the airport in New Orleans, and we stopped to eat pizza before driving to Baton Rouge. This had been Alex's first plane ride, and after time on two planes with a layover between, then sitting in a restaurant and sitting for an hour-long car ride, he was wound up and eager to explore.

We got to my home in the early evening. It was still light outside, and it was humid, though it wasn't raining at that moment.

When Alex got out of the car, it was as if he were unleashed. I got out and led the way to unlock my door while Ruba began rolling their heavy suitcases. Alex ran ahead of her and up the stairs, bounding through my door. Inside, he took a few seconds to scan the room, moving around while his eyes explored every little treasure I had collected from working around the world. I could feel his energy, like a live wire in the room. Suddenly, his curious, round, hazel eyes landed on the bowl filled with shards. His eyes grew into huge circles, and then, he didn't just point—he grabbed the bowl with both hands.

"Auntie Dima, what is this?" he wanted to know. When Alex asks a question, it seems as if every muscle in his body is also asking the question with him. Everything about him looks curious and open to absorbing new information. At this moment, he looked curious and confused at once.

I stood next to him, observing the way he looked at the bowl while holding it in his small hands. It was one of those moments when time stops and the world stops spinning. I realized the significance of those glass shards for Alex, this walking mass of energy and light and curiosity who had no knowledge of his family's history. I don't know if it was because of his tender age, or if it was because of my shock, but I didn't know how to answer him; I didn't have the words to explain.

"It's just a decoration," I answered.

"But why?" he asked, still trying to understand.

"Do you like it?" I asked him, kneeling down to look into his eyes.

He paused before responding and tried to take in the absurd notion that broken glass would be on display instead of thrown in the trash. Finally, he nodded and answered, "I like it," before he set the bowl down and moved on to explore the rest of the room.

With the repeated warning to protect and maintain my glass vase and with the invention of the graduation game, the rolled magazine-diploma tied with a bright red ribbon, Tata handed me two powerful but conflicting messages about a woman's identity. One represented restriction and a suppressed voice; the other represented freedom and the chance to discover my voice. The graduation game was part of a beautiful dream that Tata had. She hoped I might satisfy a desire she once held for herself—a specific image of a woman who lived only in her mind: a woman with social status and prestige—but one she could not attain.

Yet I don't know if she understood the real, transformative power of a diploma; I didn't fully understand it myself until it was in my hands. I wonder if Tata realized that an education would open my eyes and mind to reject the concept of a perfect vase, or that I would become empowered to smash it and learn not only to live with the broken pieces but also to transform them into power. If she had realized that the two ideals, the perfect glass vase and the rolled-up diploma, could not coexist, would she have tried to protect the vase, or would she have continued to play the graduation game?

My degrees empowered me. At IBM, I discovered both a global community and a sense of home I had not experienced before. Working there for eleven years, I grew into a confident woman.

After breaking my vase, metaphorically and literally on a stage, I realized that everyone in my life, not just Tata, has been a teacher—even the people who threatened me and caused pain. They were all my teachers. Their role was to force me to lose myself in their world, to experience terror and emptiness, and to convince me that this was the norm for living. My role was to push the pendulum to the other side and, in the process, to discover myself, my voice, and my purpose.

So, in 2015, the same year Ruba earned her master's degree, I broke another vase. I left IBM and embarked on a new intertwined personal-professional path; I started a journey of entrepreneurship.

I never imagined that I could become a version of the accomplished woman I saw at my parents' party when I was fourteen; I never fully believed that this was a real path for me, even when others believed it. But when I look back on my experiences, I see so clearly that I am transformed. Today, I am dedicated to empowering and bringing out the leadership potential in individuals. My goal is to share my story with women, men, emerging leaders, and entrepreneurs and to help them shatter their own limitations and expand their potential.

I used to think that only I was walking around with limitations. But when I got into leadership roles, I learned that we all— not just people from certain countries, cultures, or religions— have limitations to overcome. It's simply a matter of recognizing them. We all face the unavoidable threat of a physical death; this is a reality. But sometimes, we also face the threat of another kind of death—sometimes, society, our community, our family, or our work environments carry expectations that blow out our internal flame. What do we need to do to protect the fire within? What do we do to ignite it, to fuel it, and to keep it burning? I don't carry out my mission merely by talking about traditional leadership practices. I talk about turning fear into power: breaking vases, picking up glass shards, and transforming them into power. The result is more self-aware and engaging leaders—and that's what we need more of.

Even with many personal and professional transformations, I still challenge myself constantly to face fears and insecurities.

With immense gratitude for the guidance I have received and still receive from many teachers along the way—some close to me and some near strangers who showed up in my life at the exact times that I needed them—I continually grow.

Sometimes, I feel I should make peace with my father, but his story of the disobedient, ten-year-old Jordanian girl who was beaten by her father in the airport in Amman always stops me. Instead, I focus on accepting the fact that he has his own vase that one day he will hopefully break. I also focus on Alex, on the next generation, and the future.

I often consider how I will explain the bowl full of broken glass to Alex in the future. He is six now, and he is still full of wonder. I imagine telling Alex, "Because of these shards, you are here today; you are a happy and healthy boy. Because of these shards, your mom is free, your Tata is free, and your auntie is free."

I imagine that one day, Alex will watch my TEDxLSU talk. He will read this book. He will learn that the cycle of abuse that suppressed women and men in our family for generations was shattered into a million beautiful pieces. That as difficult as it was, his mom, his Tata, and his auntie had the courage and power to shatter that cycle, along with all the fear and shame that it represented.

After Alex knows this story, I will explain to him that it was Uncle Anton who first told me about this cycle when I was a teenager, that he was the one who showed me life could be different than my conditioning made it appear—Uncle Anton broke the first vase. The ripple effect that resulted created a better life for me, for our mother, for Ruba, and for Alex. I will tell Alex that he keeps me hopeful that, with time, things will continue to improve for our family and also in the larger world we are a part of.

The most jagged and painful shards are also sources of immense beauty, empowering knowledge, and transformative growth. Each and every one of us has a vase to shatter; each of us has the ability to reject shame, to claim our own identity, and to pave our own path—living out loud and in the light.

Al'ilmu noor.

العلم نور

My grandmother and me

MAIN CHARACTERS

Dima's Nuclear Family

TATA	maternal grandmother
BABA	father
MAMA	mother
WASEEM	brother
RUBA	sister

Dima's Maternal Relatives by Birth Order

UNCLE QADER	mother's eldest brother who lives in Jordan
UNCLE ANTON	mother's brother who studied and lives in US, married to AUNTIE ANNETTE
AUNTIE NADIA	mother's older sister who lives in Canada, married to UNCLE SAMI
MAMA	mother
UNCLE ZAID	mother's youngest brother who studied in US and lives in Jordan

Dima's Paternal Relatives

AUNTIE MARIAM	father's distant cousin living in San Diego
UNNAMED	father's four sisters

UNCLE JAFFAR	father's brother
HUSAM	first cousin, son of Jaffar
SELMA	first cousin, daughter of Jaffar

Malek's Nuclear Family

AMO DAWOUD	Malek's father
AMTO KASMA	Malek's mother
UNNAMED	Malek's elder brother, spouse, and son
UNNAMED	Malek's younger sister, spouse, and son

Friends and Acquaintances

EM YOUSEF	Tata's neighborhood friend
MIRA	Em Yousef's daughter
BANA	Dima's best friend in Jordan
NADER	Dima's first boyfriend
EM SIMONE	fortune-teller in Jordan
JESSICA	manager at Merrill Lynch
DR. STARLING	professor at USD
STEVE	manager at IBM
DONNA	friend in North Carolina
BARRY	mentor
CATHY	speech coach

ACKNOWLEDGMENTS

To everyone who has believed in me and seen my potential, even when I could not see it myself, thank you with all of my heart. When I look back, I realize how certain individuals showed up at important moments in my life and opened me up to doing things I would not have otherwise tried. With their help, I was able to give myself permission to dream of achieving big things. Teachers, friends, and even total strangers gave me the courage to believe in myself. To Arlette Khoury, Rawan Ghawi, Leony Daides, Anne Khoury, Mirna Musharbash, LaDawnna Summers, Barry Ross Rinehart, Katie Patton Pryor, David H. Ogwyn, Jeff Norman, Teresaa Stovin, Dee Whitaker, Rose Madbak, Dr. Stephen Starling, Jenna Walker, and many, many more—thank you for being on my side, enabling me to tell my story and to become the person I am today.

I also appreciate the individuals who caused me deep pain and who have threatened my life. They, too, are my teachers. Because of them, I have a story to tell. Because of them, I am on a mission to serve—helping others to shatter their own limitations.

My deepest gratitude goes to Herpreet Singh for her coaching, developmental editing, and writing assistance. Writing this book brought up many painful emotions, but working with you was a healing experience. Thank you for creating a safe space in which I could remember the past. With your compassion and balanced style, I felt protected enough to go back to even the worst moments; you kept me grounded, feeling safe, and empowered to continue moving forward. I am fortunate to have had the opportunity to work with and learn from your creativity and wisdom. I will always be thankful to you for helping me bring life and voice to my story, making my dream of sharing it with the world a reality.

NOTE TO READERS

I am delighted that you are reading *Breaking Vases*. In addition to the stories in this book, I am excited to share two resources with you. The first is a peek into my life and work with pictures, videos, and additional content. I invite you to use the link below to access supporting materials designed to expand your reading and growth experience.

The second is an audio program, recorded in my own voice. It is designed to help you focus on breaking vases in your personal and professional life and includes a worksheet to help you identify the internal "vases of limitations" that are constraining you.

Behind the scenes photos: BreakingVases.com
Audio Program: DimaGhawi.com/breaking-vases
Join the conversation using #BreakingVases
    Facebook: Breaking Vases
    LinkedIn: Dima Ghawi
    Instagram: Dima.Ghawi
    Twitter: Dghawi

ABOUT THE AUTHOR

Dima Ghawi is Middle Eastern in her genes and a global citizen in spirit.

With two decades of experience leading cross-cultural teams, managing client relationships, and developing talent for companies like IBM, Merrill Lynch, and Intuit, Dima combines corporate expertise with her inspiring personal story to captivate and motivate audiences.

Through keynote speeches, interactive workshops, dynamic training programs, personalized coaching, and an online community, Dima shares her leadership journey with one goal in mind: to ignite others to reimagine their potential and take daring actions.

Dima speaks to the leaders, the visionaries, and the rebels who are ready to shatter their limitations.

For more information about Dima's work, visit DimaGhawi.com.

Made in USA - Kendallville, IN
75390_9780997809350
05.05.2022 0920